DIANA ON THE EDGE

By Chris Hutchins and Peter Thompson for Smith Gryphon

Sarah's Story: The Duchess Who Defied the House of Windsor

Elvis & Lennon: The Untold Story of their Deadly Feud

Athina: The Last Onassis

DIANA ON THE EDGE

INSIDE THE MIND OF THE PRINCESS OF WALES

**CHRIS HUTCHINS
AND DOMINIC MIDGLEY**

SMITH GRYPHON
PUBLISHERS

First published in Great Britain in 1996 by
SMITH GRYPHON LIMITED
Swallow House, 11–21 Northdown Street
London N1 9BN

A CIP catalogue record for this book is available from the British Library

ISBN 1 85685 122 2

Typeset by Computerset, Harmondsworth
Printed and bound in Great Britain by Butler & Tanner Ltd, Frome

CONTENTS

Authors' Note

Journalists speculate daily on the unspoken motivations and strategies of politicians and other public figures, and the psychological biography has a pedigree that stretches back to Freud. But getting members of the psychiatric and psychological professions to comment for the record on the behaviour of the most talked-about woman in the world is not an easy task. Thankfully a number of highly qualified and independent-minded experts were prepared to assist us, and we are greatly indebted to them for shedding light on the personality whose conduct has been sufficiently baffling to leave both the Queen and the Prime Minister at a loss.

Our thanks are especially due to our two principal consultants: Dr Sidney Crown, a psychiatrist and consultant to the Royal London Hospital, and Mary Spillane, the American founder of Europe's first image consultancy, Colour Me Beautiful. We are also grateful to Dr Robert Lefever, an expert on addiction and the founder of the Promis Recovery Centre for drug, alcohol and eating disorders; Dr Dorothy Rowe, one of Britain's best-known clinical psychologists and author of, among other titles, the MIND award winning *Depression: The Way out of your Prison*; Dr Dennis Friedman, a psychiatrist and medical director of the Charter Clinic; Dr David Nias, a clinical psychologist at St Bartholomew's Hospital, London; Jeffrey Masson of the University of California, Berkeley, and author of *Against Therapy*; Susan Quilliam, a psychologist and author of *Child Watching*; Dr George Dunbar, lecturer in psychology at the University of Warwick; Dr Pippa Hugo, a senior research lecturer at St George's Hospital Medical School, London; Dr Preston Zucker, associate professor of paediatrics at the Albert Einstein College of Medicine, New York; and Diane Harrison, author of *Vicious Circle*. We are also indebted to Lord Archer of Grantchester; David Montgomery, chairman of Mirror Group Newspapers; Stuart Higgins, editor of the *Sun*; the Venerable George Austin, Archdeacon of York; Claire Rayner; Auberon Waugh; Lady Colin Campbell; and a number of people close to the Royal Family, whose anonymity we are happy to respect.

CHRIS HUTCHINS AND DOMINIC MIDGLEY, JUNE 1996

Prologue

It must count as one of the most controversial dossiers compiled on a British public figure in living memory. Put together, late in 1995, by a senior member of the royal household, it apparently described an individual suffering from a personality disorder. An unnamed psychiatrist, working from a detailed briefing on the subject's life, had concluded that his 'patient' was not able to control her actions. The subject of this assessment was the Princess of Wales.

It was the clearest signal yet of how gravely concerned those closest to the seat of power were by the increasingly erratic behaviour of the mother of a future king. The content of this most delicate of reports will never be made public, but news broke of its existence just as the authors of this book were preparing an even more comprehensive and far-reaching scrutiny of Princess Diana's mental state. *Diana on the Edge* draws on detailed descriptions of her childhood and married life, the testimony of high-level sources close to both Diana and Prince Charles, and the opinions of an august team of psychiatrists, therapists and specialist experts to take an unprecedented look inside the mind of the most famous woman on earth.

The troubled Princess has never been more vulnerable than she is today. Despite a history of mental fragility – post-natal depression, self-mutilation, bulimia and alleged suicide attempts – she had, until recently, the sympathy and support of the public and a tight-knit circle of close friends. Even if, as she said herself, her husband's friends regarded her as an embarrassment and thought she should be put in a home.

The turning-point in Diana's popular fortunes came when details were revealed of her relationship with the married England rugby captain, Will Carling. Public opinion, once so unswervingly in her favour, began to turn against her, and, with so many former confidants estranged by her growing self-centredness, she found herself more isolated than ever. It was telling that in her darkest hour – the day the full and humiliating story of her friendship with

Carling broke – the only person she could turn to was her elder son, William, who was driven up from Eton to console her. It was further evidence of a detachment that had been highlighted earlier that winter when she flew to the Caribbean for a sunshine break, not with friends, but in the company of her secretarial assistant Victoria Mendham.

Her sense of isolation can only increase with her long-awaited divorce. Her single, formal tie to the Royal Family severed and her sons both away at boarding school, Diana will be left with what one expert describes as 'a tremendous void' to fill. As she stands on the edge of a challenging new existence, there has never been a greater need for Diana to confront the demons that have plagued her since childhood.

BOOK ONE

ONE

ON THE EDGE

'It's I, I, I, sung to the tune of me, me, me.'

Dr Robert Lefever, founder of the Promis Recovery Centre for Addicts

There is no suggestion that the Princess of Wales has ever had a drink problem. Nor that she has experimented with drugs. But there is mounting evidence that Diana is just as much an addict as someone who needs an injection of heroin to see them through the day. Her 'fixes' merely come in different forms. First it was bingeing and self-mutilation. Then it was public adulation, the gratitude of the sick and handicapped, exercise, shopping and travel. Even romance and love. She has been addicted to them all. Deprived of these vital stimulants, she suffers the same sort of withdrawal symptoms as an alcoholic starved of drink. She becomes depressed, tearful and then vindictive. As one addiction specialist says: 'It's I, I, I, sung to the tune of me, me, me.'

If she were a private citizen, she might well by now have undergone a course of residential therapy. Her 'rampant' bulimia alone qualified her for a stint in the sort of recovery centre where the lavatories are locked for an hour after every meal and there are bars on the windows of the ground floor to prevent escape and on upper floors to foil suicide attempts. While her self-mutilation could have led to even more drastic treatment. Some clinical psychologists still believe in administering electric shocks to the most serious cases as part of a system of reward and punishment.

In what one psychiatrist terms 'the psychologically illiterate' confines of the royal palaces, however, Diana was seen not as a suitable case for treatment but a wilful egotist whose selfishness was a danger to the future of the monarchy. However, the psychiatrist recruited by Buckingham Palace to report on Diana's condition concluded that she had a 'personality disorder' – a catch-all term often used by specialists unable to pin down a more specific problem. It was a limited response to a highly complex condition.

Psychiatrists recognize no fewer than 12 separate personality disorders and a more instructive diagnosis might have been that she suffers from Borderline Personality Disorder or BPD. This condition has been recognized for almost a hundred years, and its symptoms are uncannily familiar to anyone who has analysed Diana in depth. They include: impulsive behaviour, including overeating, or shopping binges; extremely intense but unstable relationships (often highly manipulative and dependent at the same time); a tendency to fly into rages; no clear sense of personal identity; dramatic mood swings; a fear of being abandoned (one self-help book on BPD is entitled: *I Hate You, Don't Leave Me*); suicide attempts, self-mutilation and frequent rows; regular feelings of boredom or emptiness. Later chapters will illustrate the extent to which at least some of these symptoms of BPD apply to Diana herself.

The difference between the BPD diagnosis and the conclusion that she has an addictive personality is largely a matter of definition. While addiction specialists such as Dr Robert Lefever, founder of the Promis Recovery Centre, and his former colleague, Harley Street specialist Beechy Colclough, argue that her behaviour is a result of genetic factors and merely triggered by psychological trauma, proponents of the BPD theory are more likely to lay stress on environmental effects. So childhood traumas such as sexual abuse – often involving an isolated incident not connected to immediate family – difficult relationships with parents and neglect are frequently seen as central to its development. But what both schools of thought agree on is the desperate nature of the outcome.

Diana's neediness dates back to her unhappy childhood. Her mother's departure at a psychologically crucial age due to marital breakdown left her in the care of a distant and domineering father; she grew up insecure and lacking in confidence. She became bulimic in adolescence, gorging on anything, from kippers to All Bran as she used comfort eating, followed by vomiting, as a way of alleviating her anxiety. According to psychiatrists, up to four times as many women as men suffer from BPD, and it has reached epidemic proportions in the United States, where there are said to be more than two million sufferers. Spouses of BPD victims tell of incidents in which they are hit and have objects thrown at them.

When she married into the Royal Family as a sexually inexperienced 19 year old, there was little outward sign of the poised beauty who was to charm the world. No indication that, within a few years, her popularity would outrank not only her husband but also the entire Royal Family as she became the most photographed, most written-about woman on earth.

On a seminal visit to Australia in 1984 she went on her first walkabout. In the finest traditions of the British stiff upper lip, she was given little schooling in how to handle such occasions, but by the end of the tour she was being cheered on one side of the street, while her lack-lustre husband was groaned at on the other. It was just the fix the trainee princess needed, and she learned to depend upon it. Whether it is wearing a daringly low-cut dress at a function or displaying her legs as she leaves the gym, Diana 'can sniff a camera at a thousand yards,' according to her friend the former Lotus marketing executive James Gilbey, who now works for Ford.

As the shy teenager metamorphosed into a global superstar, the fussy Sloane designers of her youth were replaced by the best-known names in international fashion. For a 21-day tour of the Gulf states in 1986 Diana acquired a wardrobe valued at no less than £80,000. In the same way the hairstylist she had used as a kinder-garten teacher was replaced. Suddenly, her crowning glory was tinted and teased by the biggest names in hairdressing. Her habits were becoming more and more expensive.

Behind palace walls, meanwhile, she was finding more sinister ways of combating her demons. On discovering that Charles was still in love with Camilla Parker Bowles, her bulimia returned in a more virulent form, this time accompanied by a disturbing new habit, self-mutilation. The cutting helped assuage her self-hatred and by releasing endorphins – substances with a similar effect to morphine – gave her a feeling of tranquillity. While Diana now claims to have beaten her bulimia and conquered her desire to cut herself, the indications are that she has replaced one set of addictions for another.

As a schoolgirl she had experienced the rewards to be gained from ministering to the sick and the lonely as part of a 'good citizenship' scheme, and, as she began to feel more and more unloved at home, Diana came to rely increasingly on the reciprocal warmth of hospital patients. So frequent have her visits to intensive-care wards, hospices, AIDS units and homeless shelters become that one specialist describes her actions as symptomatic of 'compulsive helping' – an addiction as powerful as any other.

The regularity of her visits to the gym have an almost fanatical quality about them too. Even at times when she is under enormous media pressure, for example the day rumours circulated that she was the telephone pest behind a spate of calls to the home of art dealer Oliver Hoare, she kept her appointment with her running machine. Her incessant travelling also fits this pattern. It is construed as an attempt to flee her troubles metaphorically as well as geographically. Travel, in itself, is no solution, however. As the addicts' saying goes. 'The only trouble is, wherever I go, I'm there.'

When it comes to personal relationships, the same obsessive streak shows through. The beautiful princess is no ice queen. Since her marriage turned sour, she has endured a string of doomed liaisons, engaging in a desperate search for the love and romance denied to her with her husband. What this all adds up to is an unstable force at the heart of the Royal Family. Diana's much-reported response to the breakdown of her marriage has already exposed the House of Windsor as one of the most dysfunctional families in the land. The question now is, can she survive outside it?

In public the Princess's mask has rarely slipped. Wherever she goes, she comes across as the familiar glossy Diana, with a luminous smile for everyone she encounters, but, behind closed doors at her home in Kensington Palace, she weeps the tears of a clown. Her make-up is greasepaint, her designer outfits costumes: tools of the glamour trade, used to mask the internal loneliness and fear of a woman whose capacities are stretched to breaking-point on a daily basis. At the time of her marriage to Charles her own father is said to have told the Queen his daughter would be unable to cope with her new role. Penny Romsey and Nicholas Soames, friends of the Prince of Wales, were both against the match. Even her late grandmother, Ruth, Lady Fermoy, from 1960 a lady-in-waiting to the Queen Mother, eventually made it known she opposed it too, though she never said so at the time.

Diana today is a lonely and fearful woman. Fearful of the outside world, the press, the Palace, and her disgruntled husband, but fearful, most of all, of herself. Behind the elaborate façade she presents to a sometimes uncritical public lurks the constant anxiety that her tenuous grip on her impulses will slip, and she will be exposed as sad and desperate to an extent that few had suspected.

'I think she's suffering in the sense that she's a miserable woman,' says agony aunt Claire Rayner. 'I don't think she's a happy person, but I'm not sure that she ever will be. I fear she is slightly neurotic. On one level I'm sorry for her, on another I'm irritated because she won't do anything sensible about getting herself right again. She wallows in her problems rather than trying to get hold of them and grow out of them. That's the problem. If people could say to her, it's neither clever nor attractive, and it's time to stop wallowing, and that she will not always be young and beautiful, for God's sake, it would help.

'In another few years people are going to be very rude about her. The fuss she made about this stupid business about the lumps in her thighs for heaven's sake. Even that's an indication she's obsessed with her appearance, but if she doesn't grow out of that pretty fast, this is a lady who is going to be one very, very miserable woman in her forties.'

Despite Diana's visits to her respected north London psychotherapist, Susie Orbach, an insidious paranoia appears to be taking hold. Her staff at Kensington Palace have learned to fear her temper. There were a succession of such outbursts as her divorce negotiations became increasingly acrimonious.

Diana had appeared more in control when she confronted

9

Alexandra 'Tiggy' Legge-Bourke, the nanny Charles had hired in consultation with her to look after princes William and Harry when they were staying with him. But, again, the mask hid a woman consumed by bitterness and jealousy. In a premeditated act of some callousness she walked up to the retainer at a Christmas party for royal staff and sneered, 'So sorry to hear about the baby.' It was a reference to a baseless story she had convinced herself was true: that Legge-Bourke had recently undergone an abortion. What has not previously been disclosed is that this remark was followed by a veiled suggestion that her own husband had been the father – of which more later.

Diana subsequently made the mistake of repeating this bizarre story to the Queen. It led her mother-in-law – who took her role as head of the Church of England very seriously – to make what must have been one of the most agonizing decisions she has ever taken. Four days after the outrageous incident at the Lanesborough Hotel in London, the Queen wrote to her son advising him to put an end to his marriage without further delay. She was prepared to sacrifice her commitment to the indissolubility of marriage in a desperate bid to avert what she saw as the grave danger to the monarchy posed by an increasingly unstable princess.

'There can only have been one thing going through the Queen's mind,' says psychiatrist Dr Dennis Friedman, medical director of the Charter Clinic in London, 'that Diana was becoming so much of an irritant to the whole monarchical system that it was being brought into disrepute. It also demystified it, getting it on the front pages, day after day. The Queen must have thought, Enough is enough and said, "Let's get rid of her."

'It would have been a difficult thing for her to do, both emotionally and psychologically, because although this isn't the first divorce in the Royal Family, she comes from a happy background herself. Both her parents loved her. She had no idea she was going to be Queen – as a young girl she was third in line to the throne. She was born in 1926, the year of the General Strike, in the middle of post-war hunger and poverty, and she was made a fuss of, not only by the public and by newspapers but also by her parents who loved her dearly. So she can't visualize marital breakdown in quite the same way as, perhaps, other parents might.'

The fact that Diana had gone on national television only three weeks earlier to make a series of incendiary comments on her treatment at the hands of the Royal Family can only have fuelled the Queen's disquiet. In her now notorious interview with the current-affairs television programme *Panorama*, she even included implicit criticisms of her mother-in-law. 'I would like a monarchy that has more contact with its people – and I don't mean by riding around on bicycles and things like that, but just having a more in-depth understanding.' Knowing full well how her words would be interpreted, Diana immediately backtracked. 'I don't say that as a criticism to the present monarchy: I just say that as what I see and hear and feel on a daily basis in the role I have chosen for myself.'

Relations between the Queen and her errant daughter-in-law deteriorated further in February 1996, when Diana tried to railroad the Palace into agreeing favourable divorce terms. Within an hour of leaving a tea-time meeting with Prince Charles – during which she refused to have a note-taker present – Diana announced that she had agreed to a divorce, losing the right to be addressed as Her Royal Highness in return for a number of concessions, including her retention of the title Diana, Princess of Wales. Her statement precipitated an unusually frosty response from the Queen. She instructed the Palace secretariat to issue a press release, which included the sarcastic put-down that Her Majesty was 'most interested' to learn of the Princess's claims.

When the smoke of battle had subsided and the true sequence of events emerged, it was obvious Diana's strategy had backfired badly. The saga had begun with a letter from Charles politely implying she was dragging her feet over the matter. She had responded by requesting a meeting, which was duly arranged for 4.30 pm on 28 February in the Prince's apartment at St James's Palace – a time, date and place stipulated by her.

It has since become clear that Diana planned her approach with some precision. On the morning of the meeting she drove to Eton to warn Prince William that a divorce announcement was imminent. On her way back to London she pulled into the car park of a pub to call Prince Harry on her mobile phone at his school, Ludgrove in Wokingham, to prepare him for the following day's headlines.

Since there were no independent witnesses, and as neither

Charles nor Diana have talked openly about what took place that afternoon, one can only surmise over what happened. Since her own statement made it clear that she was to lose her HRH status, this must have been made plain to Diana by the Prince. And since the Queen went out of her way to make it known that her retention of the title 'Diana, Princess of Wales' was only 'interesting', thereby unconfirmed, one can safely assume that this was the name by which she told her husband she wanted to be known. Given Charles's bumbling, non-committal manner when in a corner, it is likely that he would have said that he could see no objection to her request. Similarly, her assertion that she was to remain at Kensington Palace, with an office at St James's Palace, would have been one of her demands, although Buckingham Palace certainly would not confirm that royal assent had been given.

When she was setting up the meeting, she made it clear to Prince Charles that she was terrified of its conclusions being leaked. And yet, within an hour of the end of the resulting negotiation, she had instructed her press spokeswoman, Jane Atkinson, to put out a statement of enormous *gravitas* through the Press Association. But even as Atkinson travelled back to her husband and two children in Chiswick, west London, the Palace was formulating its dismissive response to a pre-emptive strike that would have caused grave offence to the Queen. These are matters that are normally discussed in detail at the highest levels. Not only would the Queen have to be consulted but also Privy Councillors and the Prime Minister himself. Even Commonwealth leaders would have expected to be given advance notification of the divorce arrangements.

Despite the immediate repudiation of the terms by Buckingham Palace, Diana stood firm. And, with the Princess's demands now in the public eye, her lawyers, Mishcon de Reya, picked up the ball and ran with it. They fired off a letter to Charles's solicitors, Farrer's, demanding that the points made in the Princess's press release be confirmed. Predictably, Charles's side refused.

At this stage there was plenty of evidence that Diana was feeling the pressure. There had been a poignant incident outside the home of her psychotherapist, Susie Orbach, when she had cried helplessly for a full minute after running to her car with four photographers in pursuit. It had clearly been an emotional session, and, close to tears, as she emerged from Orbach's house, this was one occasion when she could have done without the cameramen's attentions. Pursing her lips she broke into a jog, which became a sprint as the paparazzi gave chase. When she reached her car, instead of climbing inside, she stood beside it sobbing uncontrollably, a picture of desolation.

Photographers had not seen anything like it since the day in 1993 when she confronted freelance snapper Keith Butler as she left a Leicester Square cinema with her sons in tow. To the amazement of observers she ran up to Butler, thrust her face into his and, clenching her fists, shouted, 'You make my life hell,' before brushing away tears and marching off. Although he took the brunt of her anger on that occasion, Butler has never verbally abused her. With others she has not always been as fortunate. 'Just because you're a f****** princess' is a cry she has heard more than once when driving off too soon for the class warriors among the paparazzi.

The Princess told Martin Bashir, the television reporter plucked from obscurity to conduct the *Panorama* interview: 'I still, to this day, find the [press] interest daunting and phenomenal, because I actually don't like being the centre of attention. When I have my public duties, I understand that when I get out the car I'm being photographed, but actually it's now when I go out of my door, my front door, I'm being photographed. I never know where a lens is going to be. A normal day [I] would be followed by four cars; a normal day [I] would come back to my car and find six freelance photographers jumping around me.'

It is significant that she identifies those who harass her as 'freelance' photographers – even under the stress of the interview she doesn't lose sight of the need to court the full-time staff professionals who are more vital to her long-term interests.

She went on: 'Some people would say, "Well, if you had a policeman it would make it easier." It doesn't at all. They've decided that I am still a product, after 15–16 years, that sells well, and they all shout at me telling me, "Oh, come on, Di, look up. If you give us a picture I can get my children to a better school." And you know you can laugh it off. But you get that the whole time. It's very difficult.'

By this time Diana was convinced that her emotional reactions to the constant media attention were being closely monitored by 'the enemy', the Palace old guard she herself said considered her 'unstable' and 'emotionally unbalanced'. When she was asked on *Panorama* whether she 'really' believed that a campaign was being waged against her, she replied with an emphatic, 'Yes, I did, absolutely, yeah . . . I was the separated wife of the Prince of Wales, I was a problem, full stop. [It had] never happened before. What do we do with her?'

In a bid to clarify the scale of the threat she posed, a senior member of the royal household – who has never been identified – commissioned the psychiatrist's report, based on a briefing on her 'impulsive and tempestuous behaviour'. Forensic psychologist Dr Eric Shepherd, founder of the Investigative Science consultancy, is concerned about its findings, given that psychiatry is an extremely subjective area of medicine.

Whatever the evidence, all is not well with the Princess of Wales, something well illustrated by her daily routine. Her twin passions of fitness training and comforting the sick have led to her being described by image consultant Mary Spillane as a 'cross between Demi Moore and Mother Teresa'. It was on the day of her no-holds-barred television interview that the conflicting aspects of her personality showed themselves most clearly. 'She was the power woman going to the gym in the morning, the beleaguered nun on television and the fairytale princess in the evening,' says Spillane. 'No wonder she's so messed up.'

TWO

SHOWDOWN ON TELEVISION

'In my opinion the suggestion that she was speaking from the heart seems absurd.'

MARY SPILLANE, IMAGE CONSULTANT

It was the most sensational royal broadcast since King Edward VIII went on the BBC's Home Service to announce his abdication in 1936. The film had been prepared in conditions of unprecedented secrecy. Even the then chairman of the BBC, whose wife is a lady-in-waiting to the Queen, was not told until a transmission date had been set. But, unlike Edward VIII, this royal was not about to go into self-imposed exile. The exclusive audience the Princess of Wales had granted to BBC television's documentary series *Panorama* may only have been intended for consumption within her homeland, but her shocking revelations were screened around the world. Right up to the moment the interview went out, few had the slightest inkling of quite how far Diana was prepared to go.

The following morning's newspapers were filled with details of her admission of adultery with an army captain, the doubt she expressed over Prince Charles's suitability to be king and her distress over his long-running affair with Camilla Parker Bowles. Other pages were devoted to her full and frank admission that she had suffered from bulimia and engaged in self-mutilation. She depicted herself as a wronged wife, loving mother and Kensington's answer to Mother Teresa. Her soundbites were picked up and published in just the way that she might have hoped, and a poll taken the following day showed that 72 per cent of the public thought she had been treated badly by the Royal Family. Once again Diana had demonstrated her genius for generating favourable coverage.

What was not exposed, however, was the scale of her colouring of events, the extent of her selfishness with regard to her children's welfare and the telling linguistic subtleties buried in her answers. A detailed analysis of her interview, drawing on the opinions of a broad spectrum of specialists, yields a very different interpretation from the one accepted in its immediate aftermath.

Perhaps the most worrying aspect of the whole exercise was the way her son William was brought into her war of nerves with 'the enemy'. Many feel she made some statements with insufficient thought for their effect on the children.

What everyone agrees about is that the exercise was meticulously planned. It was widely believed that she had been given sight of the questions beforehand and that she was able to veto any reference to her relationship with Will Carling. Her responses seemed coached, and her wardrobe and make-up were carefully chosen in consultation with the *Panorama* team. She showed the film crew a selection of clothes and asked them to choose the outfit that would provide the best on-screen balance for her skin tone. In the words of the fashion editor of *The Times*, she wore 'an understated black two-piece suit, a long-line, double-breasted jacket with matching short skirt and a white silk top'. This was clearly a woman who meant business.

Despite this attention to detail, however, she looked more frightened rabbit than regal swan. 'She was not made up for television,' says image consultant Mary Spillane. 'The make-up was all wrong, so she looked vulnerable and exposed. It was very unprofessional, just too light and too simple. She had very black eyes because she likes to highlight her eyes with either a blue line or a black line and uses very little foundation. She uses too little for television, and so she looked shiny. She also blow-dried her own hair, and the result was far from perfect. There were wedges on the side that weren't quite finished.

'There was very little synergy between what she had to say and what she was wearing. She dressed like a nun in black and white, which she never wears normally. It was quite inappropriate. She would have looked far more comfortable if she had worn something softer in tone. It was just far too hard, and therefore she looked far more vulnerable and less on top of things than she sounded. I would have put in something far more relaxed. Not a suit. But perhaps an easy-knit, long jacket of some sort and loose-fitting trousers. Something far more casual and in softer colours, like the beiges and camel that she looks lovely in. She also looks very feminine and soft in blue.

'As it was she looked beleaguered, very much the royal trouper, as if she had a job to do. On the other hand she wasn't trying to look totally in charge to the public, and she wanted to win some sympathy. And by wearing a suit she avoided the clothes being seen as a fashion statement.'

There was nothing cosmetic, however, about the verbal exchanges between the Princess and Martin Bashir during one of the most controversial interviews ever shown by the Corporation. It attracted a record audience of 22.8 million viewers in Britain alone and won for her inquisitor and his producers a clutch of prizes, including the prestigious British Academy of Film and Television Arts (BAFTA) award for Best Talk Show.

If anyone deserved an Oscar, however, it was Diana herself. While the interview may not have been the toughest of journalistic grillings, she showed consummate skill in deflecting any questions that probed her dark side. She reserved her most manipulative ploy to transform an admission of adultery with Hewitt into an expression of her loving nature. In answer to the most incendiary question of all: 'Where you unfaithful?', she replied: 'Yes, I adored him. Yes, I was in love with him. But I was very let down.' In the space of three brief sentences she had turned her confession into an illustration of her finer qualities and ended this verbal somersault with an appeal to the sympathies of her audience. It was classic Diana.

The thorniest issue was always going to be journalist Anna Pasternak's *A Princess in Love*, the syrupy account of Diana's love affair with James Hewitt, written with the treacherous captain's full cooperation. 'He'd rung me up ten days before it arrived in the bookshops to tell me that there was nothing to worry about, and I believed him, stupidly,' said Diana. 'And then, when it did arrive, the first thing I did was rush down to talk to my children.'

Whether or not she actually admitted the affair to her sons, she did not say, but it must have been clear to them that she was in some distress. 'William produced a box of chocolates and said, "Mummy, I think you've been hurt. These are to make you smile again,"' she said.

'It's all a bit odd, really, that he should have a box of chocolates handy when she is explaining this,' says Dr George Dunbar, lecturer in psychology at the University of Warwick, 'and there's a little sniff at the end, which seems to say, "OK, you can challenge me on this, but I'm ready to defend it," as if she's expecting to be challenged.'

Bashir had begun this, the most sensitive part of their exchange, by gently asking her to describe the nature of her relationship with 'a Mr James Hewitt'. 'That's a marked use of the indefinite article, and so it would be reasonable to interpret it as having meaning,' says Dr Dunbar, author of *The Cognitive Lexicon*, a study of words and their meaning. 'Bashir here is negotiating face with Diana. He doesn't want to encroach on her face – the way she wants to be seen – by suggesting more current intimacy with Hewitt than she might be comfortable with.'

Bashir then asked her what the nature of her relationship had been with the army officer, long known to have been her lover. 'He was a great friend of mine at a very difficult, yet another difficult time,' she said, ensuring that no one was in any doubt that her life was a bed of nails. Then she added of her soldier boyfriend: 'And he was always there to support me.' Allowing no pause for the interviewer to remind her of the question, she turned on Pasternak's book, in which Hewitt had exposed so many embarrassing details of their relationship.

'I was absolutely devastated when this book appeared,' she said, 'because I trusted him, and because, again, I worried about the reaction of my children.' The double standard here is very obvious. Any suggestion of a harmful effect on her children is nullified when it concerns disclosures she makes, but they are cited as victims if a third party has offended her.

Other references to William expose a relationship with the heir-but-one to the throne that is something of a minefield. 'There's no doubt there's loving and quite a genuine care,' says Dr Dunbar, 'but there are a few things that seem slightly unusual. First of all William's future role is emphasized repeatedly in the interview. Now this may just be because it's significant in terms of what's being discussed. But one would want to think about who benefits from the role being emphasized. And when you think about that, there's an extent to which Diana is a beneficiary.

'So he's in play in the contest between Diana and Charles in a slightly instrumental kind of way, as if Diana sees William as an instrument for her. Now I wouldn't want to put this too strongly, but William is someone she can use to support her own role, because she's the mother of the future king or even the next king, which is clearly an idea she's not unattracted to.'

Diana admitted on the programme that she had told William that his father's affair with Camilla Parker Bowles was a factor in the marriage break-up, and while she still loved 'papa' she could not live under the same roof as him.

'When she was asked what effect this had on William, she came back with no clear answer, just a cliché, calling him a "deep thinker",' says Dr Dunbar.

'She may be simply protecting him and not wanting to talk in detail about his reaction, but it does raise the question of whether she actually understands how he feels. It's possible that she doesn't give a clear answer because she doesn't really know and isn't as close to him as she'd like us to think. Then she talks about putting it to him gently, "without resentment or any anger", so she's turned the question back on to herself.

'There's another slightly odd passage where she's asked how the separation announcement affected the children, and she talks about how it had "a huge effect on me and Charles" and says, "the children were tucked away at school."'

William and Harry crop up again in one of her most eccentric remarks, where she talks about taking them to see AIDS patients but telling them they were suffering from cancer. 'It suggests that she views AIDS victims as being taboo,' says Dr Dunbar, 'and implies, on the one hand, a lack of deep sympathy and, on the other, a lack of understanding. It's a slightly odd view of how you would teach children about what it's like to be an AIDS patient. The disguising of what's actually wrong with them is a bit strange. Even if she didn't want to discuss sex she could have described it as a disease of the immune system. A similar oddity occurs when she talks about "battered this and battered that", a reference she made to women and children who've suffered physical and mental abuse. Again, there's a slight suggestion that there's a lack of empathy with these people.'

It was a nuance that clearly was not picked up by the public at large. Within weeks of the programme going out, she claimed to have received 6000 letters 'from women suffering on their own, in shelters or with bulimia or anorexia, or just desperately unhappy with their lives'.

There are three other main themes to Diana's agenda in the interview: a desire to blame third parties for her troubles; a determination to convey a particular range of personal qualities to the audience; and, paradoxically – in the context of a blatant image-boosting exercise – a need to persuade people that she was not interested in self-promotion.

The most obvious feature of the interview is her keenness to portray herself as a victim. There are some obvious examples of this. When she discussed her treatment at the hands of the media, she claimed: 'I've never encouraged the media . . . now I can't tolerate it because it's become abusive, and it's harassment.' On bulimia, she said she was 'crying out for help, but giving the wrong signals, and people were using my bulimia as a coat on a hanger'. On the discovery that her husband was having an affair with Mrs Parker Bowles she said, 'It was pretty devastating . . . a feeling of being no good at anything and being useless and hopeless and failed.' And, finally, she was a victim of plotting by allies of Prince Charles. 'Friends on my husband's side,' she said, 'were indicating that I was, again, unstable, sick and should be put in a home of some sort . . . I was almost an embarrassment.'

As Dr Dunbar says: 'In general, she's viewing herself as passive, and there are a couple more examples of this in relation to her public duties. She said she was "compelled" to perform and follows this word with a sniff. Later on she said she was "pitched out front".

Here she's drawing away from the image of being responsible for public self-promotion. Somebody else is putting her out front.

'She's obviously also very concerned not to be viewed as unintelligent, unstable or sick. Near the beginning of the interview, she said, "Well, it [post-natal depression] gave everyone a wonderful new label – Diana's unstable and Diana's mentally unbalanced. And, unfortunately, that seems to have stuck." Elsewhere she said she was seen as "stupid" after making the "grave mistake" of telling a child that she was as "thick as a plank". She'd be very sensitive to being described in that way. She's concerned to correct that aspect of her "face" as she sees it.

'She was asked about treatment she had received for post-natal depression and replied: "I received a great deal of treatment." That's a kind of a strange reply because she doesn't really answer the question at all. I wasn't sure what to make of it because I don't know whether she was ill or not, but one possibility was that she wasn't actually clinically ill. This is just the way she's portraying it. I don't know what evidence there is that she was ever clinically ill. The other explanation would be that she might be concerned with her "face", not wanting to talk about having been given drugs, for example. So there are different possibilities there.

'She just doesn't answer the question at all. There's a sniff in there. I'm not sure how to interpret these sniffs, but they do seem to mean, "This is something I'll defend if I'm challenged but don't challenge me." And then she goes on, "But I knew in myself," and that's to move the topic along herself, taking it away from the direct question.

'If it were post-natal depression, I would have thought there was very clear and direct treatment that she'd get medically, and she wouldn't be relying on the Royal Family who she's blaming there.'

The Bashir interview was also an opportunity for Diana to extol her virtues. Dunbar cites three examples. Firstly, she says she is a person who can give love: 'I lead from the heart not the head. . . . Someone's got to go out there and love people and show it.' Secondly, a mother who could teach her sons to give love: 'I want them to have an understanding of people's emotions, people's insecurities, people's distress and people's hopes and dreams.' And, finally, a woman forged by circumstance: 'Here was a strong woman doing her bit and where was she getting her strength from to continue?'

But it was her attitude to Charles that highlighted Diana's enduring bitterness at the breakdown of her marriage. She did her best to disguise her true feelings by peppering the interview with ostensibly neutral or even affectionate references to 'Charles', 'my husband' and, on one occasion, 'papa', but there were plenty of linguistic give-aways to their real nature.

'In terms of her relationship with Charles, there seems to be quite a lot of hostility,' says Dunbar. 'It is carefully measured in places. When she was asked who was responsible for the changes that diminished her role, she replied, with a big intake of breath, "Well, my husband's side were very busy" – and then there's a bit of a pause – "stopping me." The intake of breath means she's thinking very carefully about how to reply. She adds the "stopping me" at the end, as if she started off with a relatively mild approach and then thought, I can go a little bit further here, and she becomes more direct.

'All the way through there's a presentation of her face as being isolated, alone. This way she wants to be seen almost as a victim, and she would attribute responsibility for that to the attitude of the royal household. When she was asked about the Royal Family's reaction to the news that she was expecting a boy – the all-important male heir – that was a chance she had, if she was interested, to say warm things about the Royal Family, because they're bound to have done something that was very positive at that time.

'Her response isn't very direct. She doesn't accept what Bashir is offering, and she takes it back to herself – "It had been quite a difficult pregnancy, I hadn't been very well throughout it." She's concerned not to allow the Royal Family and Charles's side to be presented positively.'

But whatever Diana's feelings may be towards the Royal Family as a whole, there are signs that there is at least one member of it to whom she feels subservient. 'There are occasionally points where the register of her voice changes slightly,' says Dunbar. 'She has a way of raising the pitch and reducing the volume. When she mentions the Queen, for example, she sort of fades away. There's an emotional reaction there. I wouldn't say she is intimidated, but there is certainly respect there, even awe.

'Charles, however, is the person with whom she most often contrasts her own face. It is significant that, more than once, opportunities that are offered to promote his face are passed up. That this is a contest between them in her eyes is made fairly explicit when she talks about "the game" and "confusing the enemy".

'When she's asked whether Charles really thought she was an embarrassment, she shows some reluctance to discuss this directly. She could have used the question to soften her criticisms of Charles, it was an invitation really to do that. The use of the word "well" at the beginning of her answer there signals that she is not accepting the invitation directly, and another long breath suggests a moment is being taken for reflection before answering. Her choice of reply suggests hostility towards him, so this opportunity she's been given to care, if you like, for his face is spurned, and it's almost implied in her answer that he'd orchestrated the criticism, alluded to in the previous answer, that he was hurting her.

'When she's asked, "Who is the enemy?", she replied, "Well, the enemy was my husband's department." Again, there's a long pause before she starts to speak and another after the third word of the reply. When she comes to the word husband, that word is devoiced – like a whisper. The pausing suggests deliberate and conscious reflection, the devoicing suggests emotion, together they suggest a deliberate and measured disclosure. The key passage comes when she expresses her views about who should be king, and, although she does not say so directly, her answer strongly suggests that she might believe that William should succeed directly.'

BASHIR: 'Do you think the Prince of Wales will ever be king?'

DIANA: 'I don't think any of us knows the answer to that. And obviously it's a question that's in everybody's head. But who knows? Who knows what fate will produce, who knows what circumstances will provoke?'

BASHIR: 'But you would know him better than most people. Do you think he would wish to be king?'

DIANA: 'There was always conflict on that subject with him when we discussed it, and I understand that conflict, because it's a very demanding role, being Prince of Wales, but it's equally more demanding role being king. And being Prince of Wales produces more freedom now, and being king would be a little bit suffocating, and because I know the character, I would think that the top job – as I call it – would bring enormous limitations to him, and I don't know whether he could adapt to that.'

BASHIR: 'Do you think it would make more sense in the light of the marital difficulties that you and the Prince of Wales have had if the position of monarch passed directly to your son Prince William?'

DIANA: 'Well, then you have to see that William's very young at the moment, so do you want a burden like that to be put on his shoulders at such an age? So I can't answer that question.'

BASHIR: 'Would it be your wish that when Prince William comes of age that he were to succeed the Queen rather than the current Prince of Wales?'

DIANA: 'My wish is that my husband finds peace of mind and from that other things follow, yes.'

'She expresses the wish that Charles will find "peace of mind",' says Dr Dunbar. 'Now that could be what she means, but it could also express her wish to retain good faith and honourability for herself, while, nevertheless, still dealing the blow to Charles when she adds, "and from that other things follow". If that's correctly interpreted as an attack on Charles, then it's probably deliberate, given the careful measurement of the criticisms I've already cited.

'Taken together, the consistent reluctance to promote a good face for Charles, the carefully measured critical disclosures and the apparent final attack are all evidence of her hostility towards him.'

Dr Dorothy Rowe, one of Britain's best-known clinical psychologists and author of, among other titles, a MIND Book of the Year award winner, *Depression: The Way out of your Prison*, argues that there was a destructive streak in how Diana chose to deal with the matter of Charles's right of succession. She explains: 'If somebody asks you a question about a third person, and you just answer completely truthfully about how you see that person and then you realize that you've done that person a disservice, just by being truthful, you have the opportunity to amend your answer. But she didn't, and this was one of the questions she would have known she was most likely to be asked.'

The conflict with Charles is also evident from the extent to which he is blamed by her for a succession of unpopular acts. She made it clear that it was Charles, not her, who insisted on them attending public engagements separately; he who asked for a separation; he who wanted a divorce. When Bashir asked her what effect her cooperation with the Andrew Morton book, *Diana, Her True Story*, published in 1992, had made on her husband and the Royal Family, she admitted to thinking they were 'shocked, horrified and very disappointed'. But, asked if she could understand why, she fired back: 'I think Mr Dimbleby's book [*The Prince of Wales*, with which Charles had cooperated] was a shock to a lot of people and disappointment as well.'

'Again, in each case she's coupling her face to Charles's, comparing them and showing herself to be relatively passive compared to him,' says Dr Dunbar. 'She wants to be viewed as the goody. Throughout the interview, Diana negotiates a narrow path between criticism and disloyalty. So she's quite prepared to make critical comments about Charles, but she doesn't want to be seen to be isolating him, separating him from things he couldn't be separated from. At one point she starts saying, "my boys", and quickly corrects herself to say, "our boys". The first person singular would have been a bit more exclusive and hostile, she toned it down.'

This consistent need to blame others is a worrying characteristic, according to psychiatrist Dr Sidney Crown, a consultant to the Royal London Hospital: 'When you get that you know you're in for trouble. It's not necessarily a persecution complex, but it's a sign of someone who's very uninsightful, that is they have no insight into, or understanding of, themselves. They are constantly saying, "It's all my employer's, or my school teacher's, or my wife's, or my husband's fault." People ask in which way are we different from animals. One of the soft replies, which is correct, is that we have the capacity for self-reflection, which we can't assume animals have. If people lack that to any significant degree, then they don't develop as individuals. They may develop in the public eye, the public can push them up into being idols, but as individuals they don't develop. So that would be a big danger.'

The pattern is all too familiar to anyone who has had the opportunity to examine the lives of rock stars at close quarters.

Surrounded by acolytes, the pampered celebrities are cushioned with love, and there is no place for criticism. American psychiatrists often refer to it as 'the Elvis Presley syndrome'.

'If Elvis came down for breakfast in the morning and told the employees who were his paid friends and constant companions that he didn't like the colour black any more, they'd all agree to the extent that if they had black cars they'd go out and have them resprayed,' says Henri Lewin, the hotel magnate who presented the singer's shows in Las Vegas. 'It was a totally unreal existence, which resulted in him living in a permanent state of delusion. He was never allowed to see that he was wrong. If he made a mistake, someone else was blamed, so that his morale never suffered.'

Diana appears too fragile to accept a measure of fault and so apportions blame to other people. But Dr Dorothy Rowe believes that, in Diana's case, the need to blame others in public stems from her need to maintain her self-esteem. 'Because she's someone who sets standards, she wants to do good, to make something of her life,' she says.

However, Dr Rowe believes that in private Diana probably does blame herself when things go wrong. 'When she retires [goes home], when she can't face the world, she's blaming herself for disasters,' she says. 'She turns against herself. She hates herself, and that's the way in which a person becomes depressed. One in seven women are clinically depressed. Most people suffer a period of depression at some point in their lives, and, like most of us, she does have the capacity to become depressed. The only people who don't have that capacity are psychopaths.

'When anyone asks the question, "Why did this happen?", there are three possible answers. Either it was my fault, somebody else's fault, or it happened by chance. Now if you believe that we live in a just world – and that's what all religions teach – if you believe that everything works out in the end, and that the good are rewarded and the bad are punished, then in a grand design, nothing happens by chance. But a lot of people can't live with that degree of uncertainty: either, "It was my fault" or, "It was someone else's fault."

'Now, if you say, "It was my fault," and tell it to yourself harshly enough and regularly enough, you become depressed. If you say it was somebody else's fault, you become paranoid, so if you are somebody who cannot live with the uncertainty of knowing that in this world anything can happen, you will alternate between paranoia and depression and that's what comes out in Diana's *Panorama* interview.'

Nicholas Soames, a government minister and close friend of Prince Charles, had no doubt which mental state was uppermost in Diana's mind. Within minutes of her interview being screened he told the *Newsnight* television team that the Princess's performance had been 'toe-curlingly dreadful' and that her claims that her mail had been intercepted and her phones tapped showed she was in the 'advanced stages of paranoia'.

Dr David Nias, a senior clinical psychologist at St Bartholomew's Hospital in London, is not convinced by Soames' admittedly off-the-cuff, diagnosis, however. 'She said visits abroad would be blocked. Now was this paranoia or was it true?' he asks. 'Paranoia is having delusions that people are, for example, plotting against you, which have no foundation in fact, are purely a figment of the imagination. But she may be speaking the truth, in which case it's not. In making a diagnosis of paranoia you have got to do the detective work.'

What is certain, according to Dr Nias, is that the sweet-toothed Soames was overegging the pudding. 'If she was in the advanced stages, then she'd be a hundred times worse,' he says, brandishing a copy of Dr Peter Chadwick's *Understanding Paranoia*. 'It builds up to a crescendo. This book talks about a man who believed he was the devil, and to save the world from himself he had to commit suicide. He threw himself under a bus on the King's Road, and when he was put in the orthopaedic ward on the top floor of Charing Cross Hospital, he tried to throw himself out of the window.'

At least one aspect of her behaviour does, however, have shades of delusion. Oliver Hoare, after being advised by police that Diana was behind the spate of nuisance phone calls to his home, spoke to the Princess, only to be told that she was not the culprit. 'I know she made those calls,' he confided to his driver Barry Hodge, who would later pass on what he knew of her relationship with Hoare to the *News of the World*, 'the police know she made them, she's the only one who doesn't seem to realize it.'

'That's coming into paranoia,' says Dr Nias. 'Part of the criteria for making a diagnosis of paranoia is that there's a lack of insight. It's like our dreams. We don't remember what we dreamt last night, even though it was very real at the time.'

But if it isn't paranoia, then which condition best describes Diana's state of mind? Dr Nias says that of the 12 different personality disorders recognized by the medical profession, Borderline Personality Disorder would probably be 'the closest one could get to her'. He adds: 'But the patients who have that are so much more extreme. To me there's a clear-cut difference between them. In my opinion she would not have been able to do something like the *Panorama* interview if she was a serious case.'

Indeed, in many ways, her performance was one of great sophistication for a woman under such great stress. This comes as no surprise, given the impressive list of names of those mooted to have helped in her preparation for media appearances over the years: Lord (Richard) Attenborough, director of the Oscar-winning *Gandhi*; Sir David Puttnam, producer of *Chariots of Fire*; and Sir Gordon Reece, the man credited with turning the then plain Margaret Thatcher into an electoral proposition.

'She must have had serious coaching for every aspect of that interview,' says Mary Spillane, who has advised politicians on presentation on both sides of the Atlantic, 'and, in my opinion, the suggestion that it was just her speaking from the heart seems absurd. There were soundbites prepared, and questions had been thought through. She kept coming back to recurring themes. She had obviously been advised on body language, holding eye contact, tilting the head to show compassion and empathy, the timing and everything. It was a very polished performance. Very professional.'

Only when that performance is put under the linguistic microscope does the extent of her evasiveness become clear. No fewer than 34 of her responses begin with the word 'well'.

'I looked at the "wells", and there are three different kinds,' says Dr George Dunbar, 'and I've roughly categorized them. There are quite a few that are in fairly unimportant categories, where she's just correcting herself, or where she's just responding to being asked a follow-up question. That's quite an ordinary way to respond, and that would account for a good third of them.

'But there are at least a dozen fairly clear examples where she disagrees with something in the question, or a presupposition, or an attempt to change the topic, or something like that. She won't accept it. There is also a number of "wells" where she doesn't directly answer the question, and where, if you look at it in the context, it might even be that she's evasive. What that suggests is that she's fairly positively trying to control the conversation. She's not just passively accepting things, she actually has a view on how things should unfold.'

A good example of this occurs when she is asked about her short-lived retirement from public life in December 1993. Bridling at the suggestion that this meant she had spent 12 months in idleness, she used the 'well' to correct the direction of the conversation.

'Well, I don't know. I mean, I did a lot of work, well, underground, without any media attention, so I never really stopped doing it. I just didn't do every day out and about, I just couldn't do it.'

'It's countering presuppositions in Bashir's question which she had introduced in her previous reply,' says Dr Dunbar. 'Then she decides it's worth correcting the way the conversation's now going, because she's very concerned to be seen as hardworking.'

She makes more selective use of the expression 'yup', roughly translated to mean 'yes, so what?'

'Each time it emphasizes a commitment to a position just stated, and it suggests mild defiance,' says Dr Dunbar. 'The first time it's used is in relation to James Gilbey, when she acknowledges their recorded telephone conversation did take place. When asked whether she had had the alleged phone conversation, she said, "Yes, we did, absolutely, we did. Yup, we did." What she's doing is acknowledging that it is a problematic admission to the audience, but she's not actually accepting that it is problematic. She's saying the tape may exist, but it doesn't prove anything in terms of adultery.' She goes on to describe Gilbey as 'a very affectionate person', and Dr Dunbar reckons there is no reason to doubt her sincerity.

• • • •

Notwithstanding her own problems, Diana seemed resolved to take on the problems of a nation: 'I think the British people need someone in public life to give affection, to make them feel important, to support them, to give them light in their dark tunnels,' she said.

And, despite all the derogatory remarks she had made about the heir to the throne and the whiff of scandal she had helped to create around his family, she insisted: 'I don't feel blame. I mean, once or twice I've heard people say to me that, you know, "Diana's out to destroy the monarchy," which has bewildered me, because why would I want to destroy something that is my children's future?'

Without any apparent trace of irony, she went on: 'They don't care, people don't care any more. They've been so force-fed with marital problems whatever, whatever, whatever, that they're fed up. I'm fed up of reading about it. I'm in it, so goodness knows what people out there must think.'

Not that she had any misgivings about feeding the public yet more of Diana. Asked why she had decided to give the interview, she said: 'Because we will have been separated three years this December, and the perception that has been given of me for the last three years has been very confusing, turbulent, and, in some areas, I'm sure many, many people doubt me. And I want to reassure all those people who have loved me and supported me throughout the last 15 years that I'd never let them down. That's a priority to me along with my children. . . . The people that matter to me – the man on the street, yup, because that's what matters more than anything else.'

Millionaire novelist Lord Archer, more of a man-in-a-penthouse than a man-in-the-street, is, nevertheless, one of her most ardent supporters. He agrees wholeheartedly with her decision to speak out.

'Why should she sit there and take it on the nose?' he asks. 'She had every right to do the *Panorama* interview, and I thought it was very impressive. Charles had gone on screen seeking public affection, in a bid to show the public he was not quite the man everybody thought he was. Then he had a [Dimbleby] book brought out saying, "Here's me sitting in the hills in my kilt." God, she must have been very hurt by that.

'Let's take this at two levels. I've no doubt in my mind that she was in love with him. It must have been a shattering blow to find that he was never in love with her. First there was the famous sentence about "Whatever love is" [Charles's response to being asked whether he was in love on the day of his engagement]. Then there's the picture of them coming out of St Paul's Cathedral with him tugging at his gloves. He's more interested in getting his white gloves in the right place than this beautiful woman on his arm. And I looked at that as an author, not a politician, and I thought, You wouldn't give a damn what object was there as long as it can produce a couple of children.

'Can you imagine, on your wedding day, showing so much interest in your gloves as you're coming out of the church with the woman that you've asked to spend the rest of her life with you? That really shook me. I just looked at that picture and thought, You've never loved her, and, of course, he never did. he loved another woman. What a terrible thing to do. To marry someone when you love another woman.

'I'm not saying I lack sympathy for him, or whoever forced him into this loveless marriage. Of course I do. Especially if he loved another woman. It must be terrible, each day of your life not to get a cuddle or a chat. I understand all of that. I'm human enough to understand that, but it's not Diana's fault.'

Not everyone is quite so understanding, however. David Montgomery, chief executive of Mirror Group Newspapers, reckons that she should have shown more concern for her sons' sensibilities. Asked what question he would have asked had he been in Bashir's place, he says: 'I suppose it would have to be, "Why did you not attempt – both you and your husband – to keep this under wraps to spare the children? Like any normal couple would have done."

'Not that there would be any criticism of them transgressing, so to speak. That's neither here nor there, that happens in millions of cases. What was unusual, I think, was the fact that they didn't keep quiet about it, they expose their children to it, and I cannot understand why they would ever have wanted to do that. I think that's what I would have asked her.'

Stuart Higgins, who, as the editor of the *Sun*, could be classed as one of her greatest tormentors, concedes that she may have had some justification for taking the drastic step of doing the programme. 'She has been so let down by people around her that she has to fight her own corner,' he says. 'She has shown herself to be a very shrewd PR person, and, if it means doing the work herself, or coming up with the ideas to project herself, she is perfectly capable of doing it on her own, as she did with *Panorama*.'

The luckiest man on the night the show went out was Will Carling. While Bashir asked Diana many personal questions, any reference to her relationship with the England rugby captain, even then widely touted, was conspicuous by its absence. Carling's estranged wife, Julia, had no doubt as to why the subject was not broached. According to a friend, she said: 'The reason, of course, was that Diana knew there was a world of difference between admitting an affair with a single man and discussing whether or not you were sharing your bed with a married man. She knew the damage that raising the issue would do her, and the question was forbidden in advance.'

Despite this omission, the interview proved a critical success. 'Throughout the interview Diana remained calm, cool and controlled,' said the *Daily Mail*. 'But everywhere was the stench of revenge.'

The Times's television critic, Lynne Truss, was struck by 'those big eyes made waiflike with black kohl; the famous 15-degree tilt of the head indicating sincerity; and the occasional colouring of the royal cheeks when the name Mrs Parker Bowles was mentioned.'

And Diana, herself, was unrepentant. 'I have no regrets about doing the interview,' she said four days later. 'I have spoken to William and Harry since the programme was broadcast, and they are fine, and I am pleased that the weight of public opinion is behind me.'

It certainly was in the short term. But, as time passed, and her publicity-seeking became more urgent, it proved to have been a watershed in her previously smooth-running love affair with the British public. The interview opened up a fault line in the population as a whole, which looks unlikely ever to be closed and could, in the long term, prove damaging to the future of the monarchy itself.

Oblivious to the effects of the time bomb she had planted when it was filmed 16 days earlier, Diana spent the night of the broadcast doing what she does best, lighting up a party. In a full-length black evening dress by Jacques Azagury, one of her favourite designers, she attended a £1000-a-head gala dinner in aid of cancer research at Bridgewater House, the London home of the Greek billionaire John Latsis. She was safe among the tiny minority of adults who were not tuned in to the BBC that night.

THREE

THE WORLD IS FULL OF MARRIED MEN

'Oliver was frightened of her obsessive behaviour.'

Barry Hodge, former chauffeur to Diana's friend Oliver Hoare

Her mind in turmoil following the announcement of her separation from Prince Charles, Diana had embarked on a series of high-risk liaisons. The results were far from satisfactory. In a little more than three years she was humiliated over a spate of nuisance phone calls to the home of a married friend, exposed as something of a flirt and described as a marriage wrecker.

The setting for this fall from grace was an exclusive Chelsea fitness centre, where the membership list reads like a who's who of London high-flyers. Names such as old Etonian Oliver Hoare, a respected dealer in Islamic art; Will Carling, the England rugby captain; and Christopher Whalley, a wealthy property developer. In time all three were to fall for her combination of royal charisma and sculpted beauty.

It was Hoare, a close friend of Prince Charles, who introduced her to the Harbour Club, on the banks of the Thames, early in 1993. Conscious of her isolation in Kensington Palace, Diana had resolved to combine her fitness obsession with a search for new friends. For her, as for many others, the gym operated in many ways like a social club. The only snag was that it was a club in which many of the members were married, including Hoare and Carling.

Diana's reported disregard for marital ties is not an uncommon characteristic of women in her position, according to Dr Dorothy Rowe. 'If you followed up the life story of just about any woman in her thirties whose marriage has broken up, you'll find she's having lots of interesting affairs,' she says. 'When you're younger and going into marriage, you've still got ideas of fidelity, but in your thirties you think it doesn't really matter. When your marriage breaks up, the problem is that all the decent men are already married, so you are left with the neurotics, who don't marry, or homosexuals. So that's your choice. Unless you snaffle somebody who's between marriages, you either stay on your own, have platonic friendships with really nice homosexual men, have tortured relationships with neurotic men or meet up with some married men who are ready to stray.'

The Harbour Club seemed a most promising venue. 'She chose the most exclusive health club in the country, and the one in which she is likely to meet the right set of people: the international types, business types, people from the right background, good-looking, body-conscious folks,' says Mary Spillane.

'She doesn't want a podgy country squire with a manor house, she really doesn't. She's part of the jet-set scene, and someone who has the amount of treatments that she has is very body-centred and wants a partner who's as beautiful as she is. She probably wants a mirror-image of herself.

'I think she joined not only to have some sort of normal contact with people but also to be seen and to get some adoration for herself and her body. Her hair is never horrible when she goes to the gym. While the women sweat-hogs might have theirs up in a pony tail or wear berets to keep fringes off the face, she looks perfect.

'She also wears make-up. This is the look of the Lycra set: the look-at-me, see-how-gorgeous-I-am and how-perfectly-honed-I-am types, as opposed to the girls in baggy T-shirts. That is not to say the ones in baggy T-shirts are the overweight ones, some of the fittest ones in the gym will dress like that, but they are not there for her reasons. You have to hang out at the gym to understand this. You see the Lycra set on the treadmill, checking out who is watching them, because you have mirrors everywhere, and, out of the corner of your eye, you can see people looking at you.'

Nowhere is this more true than at the Harbour Club, the ultimate in metropolitan gyms. Mercedes, BMWs and Range Rovers fill the 80-space car park and are a reliable guide to the affluence of the members within, who make a down payment of £2600 and pay a further £100 a month for the privilege of exercising alongside celebrities such as Diana, Carling and Prince Edward's girlfriend, Sophie Rhys-Jones, on free passes. In the reception area, a polished wooden floor leads to the computerized entry system. Through the glass wall to the left can be seen the indoor tennis courts and the magnificent swimming pool, lined with tiles in the club's trade-mark dark blue. On the right is the crèche and the restaurant-bar, which serves the sort of appetizing but transistorized meals calculated to appeal to calorie-conscious members like Diana. French windows open out on to a terrace, where around 30 people can eat outside under sunshades in the summer.

Those who can resist these attractions may also work out. An industrial metal staircase leads down to the aerobics rooms and exercise areas, fitted out with the latest American-made rowing and step machines, travelators and the weights favoured by both Carling and Diana.

'She does a fairly gentle work-out,' says former member Simon Frodsham. 'She uses all the machines, but she'll only have maybe two or three goes on any one machine, before moving slowly on to the next one. It's not what you'd call terribly energetic. It's more toning than anything else.'

Her routine complete, the Princess heads not for the showers and hair dryers of the changing rooms but for the social area, where members meet over coffee. Frodsham endorses Spillane's analysis, testifying to the all-embracing nature of the Diana effect.

'I was working out one morning when Princess Diana came in,' he recalls. 'I was on one of the exercise machines, watching TV, and, on reflection, I realized that I was the only guy in the club who wasn't paying her any attention. Then, suddenly, I was aware of this powerful presence just behind my shoulder. I turned round, and there was Diana, fixing me with those glacial blue eyes. The interesting thing is that, as soon as she had my attention, she turned and walked away.'

Unfortunately for Diana, much of the adulation was of the 'look-but-don't-touch' variety. Despite her highly publicized separation, it would have taken a brave man to suggest a spot of dinner. And so, attracted by keep-fit fanatic Christopher Whalley, she found herself having to make the running. Looking up at him from the bottom of the gym's staircase, one day, she asked: 'What does a girl have to do to get a guy to buy her a cup of coffee around here?' Whalley was so stunned by the obvious chat-up line that he looked behind him to see if she was talking to someone else. She wasn't, and he proceeded to buy her the first of many *cappuccinos*, which she drank while he sipped strong, black espressos.

This episode, says psychiatrist Dr Sidney Crown, is a perfect illustration of Diana's ability to use her enormous seductive power in an ostensibly understated way, all the while being conscious of the huge impact such a request would have on one of her mother-in-law's subjects.

'If it was any two people, I would think it was just the sort of thing people do in gyms,' he says. 'Everybody likes to be friendly. People may be a bit lonely. But with her, of course, anything she says has tremendous implications. It's tremendously flattering. I believe she must have known the effect it would have. It's *her* doing it. It's not just any girl – not even a girl that's more attractive – so it's magnified dozens of times, and she would absolutely know that. In a sense I would regard that as part of her affectation. It's a throw-away remark, which is somehow a pose. I mean, her use of "a girl" – this from the most photographed woman in the world!'

Whalley was flattered by such a high-octane approach. When she offered him her private telephone number, he could hardly withhold his own, and in the succeeding weeks he was inundated with calls. Diana had her staff prepare intimate dinners for them at Kensington Palace, and she took him out to dine at San Lorenzo in Knightsbridge and Kaspia in Mayfair, two of the capital's most elegant eateries. As their relationship deepened, she spent weekends at his Yorkshire family farmhouse, in the same way she had once visited the Devon home of her ex-lover James Hewitt's mother. By November 1994 she was so smitten by her new friend that she promised to send him a signal by flashing her red nails in a certain manner when she was filmed during a charity function at the

Palace of Versailles. In return for such devotion Whalley was expected to act as an emotional crutch. On one occasion, despite the fact he was dining with a former fiancée, he was obliged to interrupt their evening by watching the television documentary, *Portrait of a Princess*. To the bemusement of his old flame, he then used her phone to call Diana and reassure her, over and over again, that she could count it as another triumph. It is a revealing insight into not only her latent insecurity but also her insatiable appetite for praise and adoration. And no one man could provide her with enough of that.

By now Whalley, who continues to see Diana on occasion, was aware that he was sharing the Princess's attentions with another Harbour Club member, the equally physical Will Carling. Although he was about to marry, Diana struck up a relationship with him shortly after she'd begun her close friendship with Whalley. Interestingly, neither man came from the sort of aristocratic background from which a titled woman could be expected to draw her mates.

Dr Crown identifies this syndrome as the 'princess/prostitute complex'. 'Because of Diana's various conflicts with her parents, she finds she cannot deal adequately in emotional terms with people who are her peers and reflect her background,' he says. 'She can deal better with people who are her inferiors. You see it particularly with gay relationships. Incredibly sensitive, marvellous people, who must go to the Elephant and Castle [a run-down district of south London] and make relationships with the toughest, roughest trade they can find.

'It's obvious she goes for the extremely physical type. They have machismo, if you like, they express their sexuality overtly. There is no reason to suppose that the people who are the most "hunky" – who everyone thinks, They must do it five times a night – are not, in fact, impotent. Again, you can't tell unless you are in the bedroom.'

As his wedding day drew near, Diana showered Carling with presents and took her sons to meet him several times at the Harbour Club. On at least one occasion he accompanied the trio back to Kensington Palace for lunch. As the couple grew closer, she even took the young princes to the Twickenham stadium to train with Carling and the English rugby team. A pattern was repeating itself:

Hewitt had given the boys riding lessons. Carling revelled in the association and was prepared to put at risk his fledgling marriage for the sake of a close friendship with one of the most sought-after women in the world. According to Carling's personal assistant at the time, Hilary Ryan, the pair phoned each other incessantly – up to six times an hour, in Carling's case, according to his itemized telephone bill. She called him Captain, and he called her the Boss. This is fertile ground for the analyst.

'I would imagine that in this particular context, where you have Will Carling coming from a fairly ordinary background and her from a very different background, that the use of the term boss was ironical,' says Dr Sidney Crown. 'She's the boss because she's famous, she's royal, she's this, she's that. Not necessarily the boss in the sense that she orders him around. I mean, she may be a bossy person, but I see her much more as an impulsive. She might say, "I want to make love tonight," but it would be in the impulsive sense rather than the bossy.' Interestingly, Diana became known as 'the Boss' by disgruntled staff at Kensington Palace soon after she moved in after her wedding.

Dr Dennis Friedman argues that it might be more to do with a sort of mutual neediness. 'I suppose he was looking for a mummy just as she was,' he says. 'People are attracted to each other because they have similar needs. And what she must have seen in him is the same helpless need that she has in herself. And what she needs is somebody to look after her, to love her and nurture her, because her mother abandoned her. I don't know anything about Will Carling's background, but he may well have had the same sort of needs and been very happy to see her as a sort of boss figure, who would comfort and compensate him for losses he had suffered in the past.'

Their relationship was to prove the most damaging of Diana's dalliances. When details first appeared in August 1995, Carling and Julia, his bride of 14 months, gave a joint interview. In front of his wronged wife, the sporting hero admitted his behaviour had been 'unforgivable'. He went on: 'My main feelings are what it has done for people around me, the people I really care about and love. It was a perfectly harmless friendship with the Princess, but I've been incredibly naïve to put myself in that position.'

It was a slap in the face for the besieged Princess, and one that would have hurt her deeply. 'I think she would have been angry and disappointed,' says Dr Friedman, 'but she sets up situations for herself in which she's going to be disappointed. People who grow up with the disappointments and rejections that she has had get into a kind of pattern and set up difficult situations for themselves over and over again.

'Most of her relationships have involved men who, in her eyes, were ideal in that they were people of status. They've all been captains of something. Will Carling, rugby captain, James Hewitt army captain and so on. And she gets attracted to those, irrespective of whether they're available or not, or whether they're suitable. Some of them have not been available and all of them have been unsuitable because they've all been in it for themselves. They might all have been officers, but none of them was a gentleman.'

Dr Crown reckons Carling was completely out of his depth. 'He suddenly woke up to the fact that there were photographers everywhere and that the whole thing had got completely out of control, and so he had to develop all sorts of strategies to try to get out of it, including dealing with his wife,' he says.

'These are the sort of things that an ordinary man never has to deal with. So I think he probably got into another area of neurology, what is sometimes called a catastrophic reaction. Rational thought goes out the window. Again, he was impulsive, and he was probably starry-eyed.'

Breaking his very public promise to have nothing more to do with her, Carling telephoned Kensington Palace to say that he would be calling round on the evening of 5 September. Instead of staying in to greet her admirer, Diana slipped out of the Palace and went to visit Joseph Toffolo, the ailing husband of her acupuncturist, Oonagh, in hospital. When the hapless Carling arrived not only was there no Diana to meet him but also photographers were in position to record his clandestine visit. The explanation he offered for his breach of trust – that he was delivering rugby jerseys for William and Harry – was met with derision.

For good measure a photographer was also on hand a fortnight later when he and Diana met at the Bimal fitness centre in Hammersmith. What might once have been construed as a mild flirtation at the Harbour Club had now taken on the status of a marriage-wrecking affair. And within a month the Carlings had announced a trial separation, never to be reunited.

Meanwhile Oliver Hoare had become a devoted admirer. For the vision in figure-hugging Lycra who greeted him during their first work-out together was a very different woman from the downcast, estranged wife to whom he had been introduced by Prince Charles.

Diana would have had plenty of justification for rejecting any advances from her husband's friend. She knew through the Palace's highly efficient bush telegraph that Hoare was supporting Charles's rekindled relationship with Camilla Parker Bowles by hosting candlelit dinners for them at his home less than a mile from the gym in Tregunter Road. Hoare's conflict of loyalties was obviously something Diana was prepared to overlook, however. Diane Hoare's ruggedly handsome husband was just the sort of man who appealed to the lonely Princess, and the stage was set for a relationship that was to embroil the pair of them in a national scandal.

Within weeks Diana began to betray the sort of obsession with Hoare that was to prove the hallmark of all her close friendships. When she celebrated her birthday at his gallery a stone's throw from her husband's office in St James's, with no other friends available it was Hoare's chauffeur, Barry Hodge, who was required to wheel in a cake, singing, 'Happy Birthday to You'. The Princess was obviously in democratic mood, for when Hodge sang the line 'Happy Birthday your Royal Highness,' she interrupted him with a laugh to say, 'No, Barry, it's Diana.' As Hodge recalls: 'She was quite squiffy from the champagne they were drinking.'

Diana's determination to glean every detail of Hoare's life even extended as far as inviting his two female assistants, Amanda and Geri, to lunch at Kensington Palace and dinner at San Lorenzo in order to question them about their employer. As her obsession grew, she bombarded him with telephone calls. 'If she only called five or six times we thought of it as a quiet day,' says Hodge. 'The sheer number of calls she made used to get Mr Hoare down. He'd cringe when the phone went off sometimes.'

On one occasion Diana was trying to contact Hoare when he

was at a business lunch in Mayfair. When she got Hodge on the car phone, she demanded to know where Hoare was and who he was with. Hodge, covering for his boss, said the only information he had was that he was lunching at a restaurant in Mayfair. It was enough for the Princess. An hour later, when Hoare returned to the car, he said, 'She managed to get me.'

The chauffeur says: 'The Princess had phoned all the restaurants in the area until she found where he was and managed to talk to him.' Hodge claims he would take up to six calls a day on the car phone from 'a mystery caller who would often try to disguise her voice by pretending to be an American or a child'. The deception was exposed when Hodge pressed the phone's redial button after Hoare had returned one of the calls. The voice that answered was clearly that of the Princess of Wales.

Embarrassing as this might have been, it was a spate of calls to Hoare's home that proved to be Diana's undoing. Whenever Mrs Hoare took a call, the anonymous caller would put down the phone without a word. But, one day, things changed. Mrs Hoare was met with a volley of abuse. For Hoare's troubled wife it had become too much to bear. In October 1993 she forced her husband to go to the police. Kensington police agreed to monitor the Hoares' line, and after weeks of surveillance, the art dealer was summoned to Earl's Court police station.

'When he emerged from the police station, he telephoned the Princess and began to give her a right dressing-down,' says Hodge. 'I heard him say to her, "It's a nightmare, I've just been to the police about the calls." Then he asked me to step out of the car. I was outside for 20 minutes while the row went on. When I got back into the car his face was white.'

Diana stuck to her story in her *Panorama* appearance when she told interviewer Martin Bashir: 'I was reputed to have made 300 telephone calls in a very short space of time, which bearing [in mind] my lifestyle at that time, made me a very busy lady. No, I didn't, I didn't. But that again was a huge move to discredit me and very nearly did me in, the injustice of it, because I did my own homework on that subject and, consequently, found out that a young boy had done most of them. But I read I'd done them all. Mr Hoare told me that his lines were being tapped by the local police station. He said, you know, don't ring. So I didn't, but somebody clearly did.'

Had Diana been able to psychoanalyse herself, she might have offered the explanation that telephone use had become second nature as it was the only means of regular contact with her mother after she left the family home when Diana was six. Instead she tried to play down the matter. Asked how many times she had in fact phoned him, she fudged the issue: 'I don't know,' she began uneasily. 'Over a period of six to nine months, a few times, but certainly not in an obsessive manner.'

Hodge, however, sees it differently. 'Oliver was frightened of her obsessive behaviour. He knew he was losing control of the situation.'

What a layman might see as a simple dispute over a matter of fact takes on a different perspective when seen from a professional viewpoint. Dr David Nias and Dr Sidney Crown explain this type of self-delusion with reference to the psychopathological concept of 'disassociation'. 'It's a serious thing,' says Dr Nias. 'It literally means that the brain goes into a sort of altered state of consciousness. It could just be that she's having elements of a more serious disorder but hasn't got the full-blown disorder. Like someone who's schizoid but hasn't got schizophrenia. They are odd and eccentric, but they're not mad. There's a world of a difference between the two. So what one can say is that she's manifesting elements of mental disturbance rather than having a mental illness. This is a stress reaction. Under stress all sorts of strange things happen, and she clearly is under stress.'

Dr Crown identifies Diana as a hysterical personality. 'The thing about people who have that sort of personality is that not only are they very demonstrative and very extrovert and very exhibitionist but they also have the ability to disassociate. It's rather like when you sit down with a chap who has an alcohol problem, and he says, "Don't worry, I'll never drink again." You know he will drink again, but he doesn't know he will. Somebody else might say he's lying, but a disassociative mechanism has just flipped in.'

He describes her refusal to accept that she had made the calls, despite the evidence that they had come from her phones, as 'perfectly plausible': 'It is a tremendously difficult grey area, that of amnesia and which part of the mind overlaps with the conscious mind. It's just like dealing with criminals. Are they lying? Or have they cut off? You just don't know. It's not mental illness. People can disassociate in the way I have described – in other words they don't know they've done something – without being mentally ill. If it was a permanent form of behaviour then, yes, you would say this is a very serious form of disorder.'

At one stage Oliver Hoare moved out of the family home. 'Oliver was staying at a very modest address in Pimlico', Hodge recalls. 'In fact it was a little housing-association flat rented by a secretary, which I always thought the Princess, on her visits, must have considered very downmarket. But at least he had done the decent thing and moved out of the marital home while the Diana storm raged.'

Will Carling's marriage was doomed to end in a messy divorce, and an uncomfortable calm has settled over the Hoare household. So what made two men, with so much to lose, risk their marriages and reputations for what they must have known from the outset was an impossible goal – a long-term relationship with the estranged wife of the heir to the throne?

To understand what drove them to do it, according to Dr Crown, we must appreciate the powerful allure of a princess at play: 'What's intrigued me very much about her dress is how she sexualizes it in her gym clothes, for example,' he says. 'I think she takes enormous trouble to make those clothes unbelievably sexually provocative. I don't think she's ever developed emotionally very far, and she probably would have had difficulty anyway. I think if she was left in complete privacy, it would be difficult. She picks the sort of people who, themselves, are quite self-centred. We have talked about their physicalness, so she doesn't start with the sort of person who would be introverted and sensitive enough to want to try to work at a relationship but is probably much keener to look at himself than to look at her. And so all these things are against her. Then, I think, media pressure comes in again, and they just can't cope with it.'

Dr Crown's observation is endorsed by no less a person than Diana herself. Asked on *Panorama* to explain why she saw her redemption in work rather than a new relationship with a man, without naming either Hoare, Carling or Whalley, she replied: 'Any gentleman that's been past my door, we've instantly been put together by the media, and all hell's broken loose. So that's been very tough on the male friends I've had.'

Press intrusion, according to Dr Crown, is not the only factor behind her inability to form lasting intimate friendships: 'Here the concept of "committal" is a very important one. In my practice about 80 per cent of the people I see are between 25 and 40. Two-thirds of them are women, and they say, "There's nothing wrong with me. I've got this job, I've got that job, I'm very successful, but I've never been able to commit myself to anybody, it always breaks up."'

It is this independent streak that is picked up by Mary Spillane. 'She has this American influence on her,' she says. 'I think she has adopted a lot of this confidence and wanting to be a strong woman thing. Remember the recent portrait she had done of herself where she told the artist, "Make me look strong"? For a British woman to say that is weird. American women love to look strong, they like this muscle definition, the Demi Moore look: very modern, very strong, very confident. A look that says, "I'm an individual, I can stand on my own two feet, I don't need a man," in-your-face stuff, which is American. Therefore the American flag sweatshirt, with the cycling shorts and the rest of it, is all part of this.

'She's part of a generation that's grown up not buying into the traditional family package [but] working, trying relationships, getting out of them, being very self-possessed, having all the help of the therapists and the treatments. It's a very self-centred existence that involves shelling out a substantial portion of income to take care of yourself and feel good and to look good. And then you have all the conveniences of modern life. You don't cook a meal. You eat out or you buy it in. It's a generational change.'

It all adds up to a style that would make her feel at home in the United States. 'She is feeling more and more isolated in her home country,' says Spillane, 'just as Fergie was when she was being attacked by the British press and public for the very things that are championed in America: for being a bit of a jerk, for thumbing your nose at the establishment. They are always fêted in America, and there are women of every age there who say, "Three cheers to them." They have a lot of American women friends as well as male friends. They are loved over there for being the way they are, warts and all, and they are encouraged to be that way.'

But will a change of geography give her more luck with men? Dr Dennis Friedman doesn't think so. 'She would never make a relationship with a man who would be right for her because she can't believe that there is anyone who would be available and stay the course, because her mother didn't, her father didn't, her nanny didn't, teachers came and went, and Charles left her,' he says.

'There isn't an ideal person because someone with dependent needs needs someone to feed into their dependency. What the one with dependent needs needs is to grow up and be independent and have an adult relationship with another human being, and she hasn't been able to achieve that yet, but hopefully she will because, as far as I know, she's having quite a bit of therapy, and I hope that it's pointing her in that direction.'

There are signs, however, that Diana herself may have lost her stomach for the battle of the sexes. 'You know, people think that, at the end of the day, a man is the only answer,' she told *Panorama*. 'Actually, a fulfilling job is better for me,' she added, laughing. So did the laugh suggest the reply was tongue in cheek?

'I think she was speaking truthfully because the job is more important to her,' says Dr Friedman. 'She wants to be a princess, she wants to be an ambassador, she wants to be on centre stage all the time, and if that's her job she's not going to give it up lightly because it satisfies a need in her, the look-at-me need. She's grown up to need people to look at her. She's an exhibitionist, and every exhibitionist has to have a voyeur; she wasn't married to a voyeur. Fergie is also an exhibitionist, she likes to be looked at and admired, and she married a photographer [Prince Andrew is a keen amateur photographer] so that worked for a while.

'Now, you see, with Diana, Charles isn't a voyeur, he's the same as she is – he's a helpless child needing to be loved because he was kicked out – out of the nursery, out of the home, far too early. He was self-sufficient at the age of four, then pushed off to boarding school, when really he wanted to go to the local school. He's an unhappy man – he's looking for something, but he doesn't know what, and so is she. That's what attracted them to each other, but at the same time it allowed the whole thing to fall apart. Neither of them had anything to give because they were both looking to take.'

FOUR

RIVALS

'What she's doing in all these relationships with men is attacking women.'

DR DENNIS FRIEDMAN, PSYCHIATRIST AND MEDICAL DIRECTOR OF THE CHARTER CLINIC, LONDON

One ghost Diana was not able to exorcize on *Panorama* was that of Tiggy Legge-Bourke, the younger woman she believed was getting dangerously close to both Prince Charles and the children. While other perceived threats could be handled with relative ease, the blameless 30 year old, who had been dubbed the young Princes' 'surrogate mother', would take a more sophisticated approach. Even as Diana wondered what to do, however, what neither she nor Legge-Bourke could have known was the extent of the backstage manoeuvring taking place to install the royal nanny as the next wife of Prince Charles, a plot the authors uncover in this chapter.

As it was, Diana was quite paranoid enough. She resorted to innuendo, spreading false rumours that the royal nanny had had sex with Prince Charles, become pregnant and then travelled abroad for an abortion. While the tale soon became the talk of their circle, frustrated when nothing appeared in print to discredit her target, Diana decided on direct action. To turn on the fun-loving, plain Jane at a society do would have diminished Diana in the eyes of her peers, so she bided her time until the day of the staff

Christmas party thrown by Diana and her husband at the Lanesborough Hotel on Hyde Park Corner on 14 December 1995. There she walked up to her quarry and said, with *faux* sympathy, 'So sorry to hear about the baby.' While these seven words were plastered all over the tabloids six weeks later, her follow-up remark, 'If you had sex with my husband, I hope you enjoyed it because I never did,' has gone unrecorded until now.

Legge-Bourke's response was predictable. 'Shocked and amazed' in the words of one of her closest friends, she slumped into a chair and had to be comforted by Michael Fawcett, Prince Charles's valet. Four days later Legge-Bourke called in the country's leading libel lawyer, Peter Carter-Ruck. While ruling out taking the Princess to court and dismissing her rantings as the actions of a 'mad' woman, according to the *Sunday Times*, she did instruct her lawyers to write to Diana's solicitors, Mishcon de Reya, demanding the allegations 'be privately withdrawn and recognized to be totally untrue'. Two days after that Carter-Ruck warned newspaper editors not to publish the story as fact.

It proved a futile exercise. The attack was duly reported, and Diana's supporters even suggested the legal manoeuvres were partly to goad the press into breaking the story. What cannot be denied is that its effect was to leave in tatters Diana's reputation as a woman more sinned against than sinning.

So what did lead such a politically astute public figure to make such a mistake? One intriguing suggestion is that, despite all the evidence to the contrary, Diana was still in love with the man she married, had convinced herself the rumour was true, and her outburst was a case of her heart ruling her head. After the divorce meeting with Charles, she let it be known to the BBC TV's royal correspondent, Jennie Bond, that it was an emotional occasion. 'She apparently said to him she had always loved him, that she had no regrets about marrying him and that she was agreeing to a divorce against her wishes,' said Bond.

This rings true for forensic psychologist Dr Eric Shepherd. 'The one thing which is now basically the issue and comes across loud and clear is that she still loves him. I'd be very surprised if she doesn't love him.'

Dr Dennis Friedman agrees. 'I think she loves him,' he says, 'but I think she's confused in her mind as to what she means by loving. I think what she actually loves is the status that she has achieved, all these kind of illusory symbols of love, metaphors for love. She was, after all, rescued from quite an unhappy childhood, a broken home, and then Prince Charming turned up, and I'm sure she just loved that and loved him because of what he represented for her. She's been very distressed and now very angry that she's been cheated out of that.

'I was also rather impressed by her use of the term "my husband" when I watched the interview. She said it in a very possessive sort of way. Admittedly she could hardly have said, "good old Charles", but there was just something in the way she said it, bearing in mind that she must have rehearsed that interview a number of times.'

Dr Sidney Crown says the ties that bind will not fall away easily. 'When people have been together for a time and shared children they can never entirely detach themselves and pretend that the other person doesn't exist,' he says. 'You can burn photographs, but you can't destroy the memories. Certainly she will have complicated feelings about him, just as he would have complicated feelings about her, and some of those feelings must be positive. When she's looking through the photograph albums, she's bound to come across pictures of happier times. And, yes, then she would feel warmth and affection towards him.

'So I wouldn't deny that she still loves him, but I wouldn't think she was committed to him in any systematic and ongoing sense. I would think it was much more of a fleeting thing. A lot of people do remarry, but too much unpleasantness has flowed under the bridge in this case. If he came along and proposed all over again, I would be surprised if she'd accept.

'As it is, she is going to miss all the trappings enormously. I think that's one of the worst things for her, because she likes all that. She could go somewhere where she is still much loved, and America is the obvious place.'

By now Diana was trapped in a complex web of relationships, in which her rivals' supporters were unified in one aim: to neutralize

her power. This battle for the romantic succession was characterized by a level of vitriol that was almost comic in its intensity. At
one point Camilla Parker Bowles was reported to have dismissed
former chalet girl Legge-Bourke as the 'hired help' and concluded:
'She may be very good at making bacon and eggs in the morning,
but she's not the type of woman you marry.'

Meanwhile members of Charles's camp, dismayed at the
growing influence of Mrs Parker Bowles, were making attempts to
discredit her in Charles's eyes and promote Legge-Bourke as her
replacement. For the chubby girl, who originally joined the staff at
St James's Palace on trial as an assistant to the Prince's private
secretary, Commander Richard Aylard, had undergone something
of a transformation. She had lost two stone in weight and, never the
smartest dresser, appeared to have had a complete make-over. In a
desperate bid to dampen down the romantic speculation the Palace
revealed that the reason for her weight loss was an eating disorder,
coeliac disease.

The first indication that a plan was afoot to matchmake her with
Prince Charles came shortly after six o'clock in the evening of
Monday, 6 November 1995, when Chris Hutchins, co-author of
Diana on the Edge, took a call from a senior member of Charles's
circle. He was summoned to an address in Belgravia and told that a
file was being prepared for the Queen, that showed Camilla Parker
Bowles to be partly behind a surreptitiously organized publicity
campaign designed to banish her public image as a dowdy
adulteress and make her acceptable as a future Queen. It was
during this meeting that the writer learned the scale of the crusade
being mounted to sideline Diana and substitute Legge-Bourke in
the nation's affections.

'Tiggy is definitely the woman many of us would like to see at
his side for the future,' the contact began. 'I have known her most
of her life, and she is eminently suitable to be the next Queen. She
is an honest, down-to-earth, country girl, and she and the Prince
share a lot of the same interests. What's more, the boys adore her,
and she's young enough for Charles to start a new family with, if he
so chooses. But, even more important, the people would love her.
Mark my words, she would be the next Queen Mother figure. She's
that sort of lady.

'As for Diana, I believe it is time that we left her alone. I have given off-the-record briefings about her before, and I've said that she is a sick woman. Today everyone knows that to be true, thanks to her brave admission on the *Panorama* programme that she'd had treatment. But I dread to think how it will all end for her if the pressure is not taken off.'

At subsequent meetings at a mansion in the West Country, the source discussed the details of the public-relations exercise allegedly encouraged by Mrs Parker Bowles.

'I can assure you that no one was more surprised than [Lady] Sarah Keswick [a long-standing friend of Charles and wife of the banker John Keswick] when the paparazzi turned up in strength for her 50th birthday party at the Ritz, because they had been tipped off that Charles and Camilla would be there under the same roof,' Hutchins was told. In the light of these revelations, it would seem that when Diana told *Panorama*, 'There were three of us in this marriage, so it was a bit crowded,' she was underestimating the degree of congestion.

But no amount of public-relations work will eradicate the humiliation heaped on both Mrs Parker Bowles and the Prince by the publication of a tape recording of one of their late-night telephone calls – immortalized by the name Camillagate. The most embarrassing passage occurred when Charles made reference to a reincarnation as a tampon.

'I think that tape was really shattering in the sense that somebody got hold of it,' says Dr Sidney Crown. 'Let me put it in a wider context: everyone has childlike bits in them. And they are acted out in private with partners. You know there are hundreds of people who dress up, and they don't talk about it. They do sado-masochist things, verbal things, where the only thing that will switch on their erections is a woman swearing at them, that sort of thing. There are all sorts of secret lives that nobody knows about.

'When Charles's most secret fantasy about wanting to be a tampon and put inside his lover is revealed to a curious world, it seems absolutely outrageous in a person who is going to be your king, but in ordinary people it honestly isn't so unusual. What it did reveal was the very infantile bit of him, his infantile sexuality. But people can live with infantile bits like that, and as long as their partner will go along with them they can still have a reasonable sex life. There is a parallel in the way some men want women to dress in a certain way for sex. The women will say, "I'm not putting on that, but I will wear that." The point I am making is that couples will play with each other's infantile bits, and it can be successful.

'The difference between ordinary people and a royal couple is that they don't get recorded discussing what they are doing. Most of us would feel absolutely shattered if it happened to us, because material like that is so private, but I think it's hard to know how people brought up in that environment would react. One does feel they are brought up not to show feelings, even to themselves, and that, combined with the sort of arrogance of a person who is going to be king, might enable him to get over it. Whether it would recur in his dreams or in his most secret life I don't doubt. I think he must have been mortified when that came out. Everyone somehow remembers it.'

Men who have fantasies will often go to a prostitute to discuss them or act them out, because they are either too embarrassed to suggest them to their partner, or she is unwilling. 'You get hookers who say, "Look, John, you can put anything on to me,"' says Dr Crown. 'I'm quoting dozens of men who say that. And often the wife will say, "Look, you go and do it with 'X' but don't tell me about it."'

As Diana's life became more and more complicated, the jockeying for position was not confined to her rivals for Charles's affections. By this time the women in the lives of her men friends were also cutting up rough. Will Carling's wife, Julia; Oliver Hoare's wife, Diane; James Hewitt's 'unofficial' fiancée, Emma Stewardson; and James Gilbey's late fiancée, Lady Alethea Saville; all had good reason to despise Diana.

As Stewardson, who had been seeing Hewitt for some months by the time he met his royal lover in 1986, said: 'Diana accused Camilla Parker Bowles of crowding her marriage. But Diana did exactly the same thing to James and me. She is being totally hypocritical over this. My relationship with James was wrecked, and she knows it. There might have been three people in her marriage, but she made sure she was the third person in my relationship with James.

'She wouldn't leave James alone, she was relentless in pursuit of him. Everyone makes out James is the total cad, but Diana caused more than her fair share of upset and hurt. For nearly four years I had hoped that James would be stronger in the end, but it was hopeless. She had him well and truly hooked. A lot of people have been very upset by how she has behaved with other people's husbands and boyfriends.'

Diana made little attempt to spare the feelings of the other women. On one occasion there was a furious row after she arrived unexpectedly at Hewitt's mother's cottage in Devon while Stewardson was there. One witness to what followed, a member of a crack anti-terrorist unit keeping protective watch on Diana, said: 'She knocked on the door, and he answered saying, "This is rather inconvenient." Diana started rather loud screaming and shouting – she had a temper like something [going] out of fashion.'

Dr Dennis Friedman says this all comes down to an unconscious desire on Diana's part to avenge herself on the mother who abandoned her at the age of six. 'What she's doing in all these relationships with men is attacking women, because most of these men are married, and it's a way of getting at the woman,' he says. 'It's because of her mother. It's her way of retaliating against what her mother did to her. She is making women suffer.'

While Diana was intimidated by Mrs Parker Bowles, a forbidding divorcee, 14 years her senior, she, at least, played a straight bat. In Julia Carling, the glamorous wife of Will, the then captain of the England rugby team, Diana met her match in cunning.

'In Camilla, Diana had somebody who played by the rules,' says psychologist and author Susan Quilliam. 'If Diana had played by the rules, we would have known nothing about the problem. The age difference between the two may only be 14 years, but it's a generation.

'Camilla is playing by the old rules, the rules literally of a generation ago. She's the Prince of Wales's mistress, and she keeps her mouth shut. Diana is playing by the rules of the new generation: "My husband cheats on me, I kick up a stink about it. I don't necessarily tell the press but I try to fight back."'

'Diana, if she had followed the old rules, would not have tried to get Charles back. She would have said, "We have a marriage." Charles too would have followed the old rules. He wouldn't have walked out on the marriage. He would have stuck by it in name. He would have given her two sons. He would have been courteous and respectful to her. They could have been quite good friends in the way that Elizabeth and Philip are: old rules. New rules: "My husband has an affair, I fight it. I make it his problem and my problem, and I try to recover our relationship by throwing myself down the stairs. I try to get his love that way – and it doesn't work."'

Julia Carling took a similar approach. Rather than abiding by the 'old rules', like Mrs Parker Bowles, she was prepared to work through the media, and that came as a shock to Diana. Quilliam reckons this is why she was so taken aback at Hewitt's behaviour too. 'The reason Diana felt so betrayed was that, while she didn't play by the old rules, she expected everyone else to. Hewitt played by the new rules, which say, "If the Princess of Wales is going to sleep with me, then I've got a right to make some money from it."

Indirectly Julia Carling was to profit from the notoriety she gained from her husband's relationship with Diana. To the chagrin of the Princess, Julia's stock rose each day the hapless Will was pilloried by more detailed reports of the affair. It emerged that she had discovered dozens of calls to Diana being charged on his telephone account. He was even accused of boasting to his team mates about sex with the Princess.

But while Julia might have had reason to feel resentful of Diana in her personal life, her television career was taking off. On the day details of her husband's royal fling dominated the front pages, the previously anonymous publicist was being fêted as Satellite Television Presenter of the Year. Like many a wronged wife down the centuries, Julia was one of the last to know the truth about her husband's affair, but the tell-tale signs would have been there, if only she had had the expertise to identify them.

In triangular relationships each party is affected, even if they don't all know about the others. In the Carlings' case Julia was not aware of the Princess's relationship with her husband until they had been seeing each other for some time, but in subtle ways she would have noticed changes in her husband's demeanour.

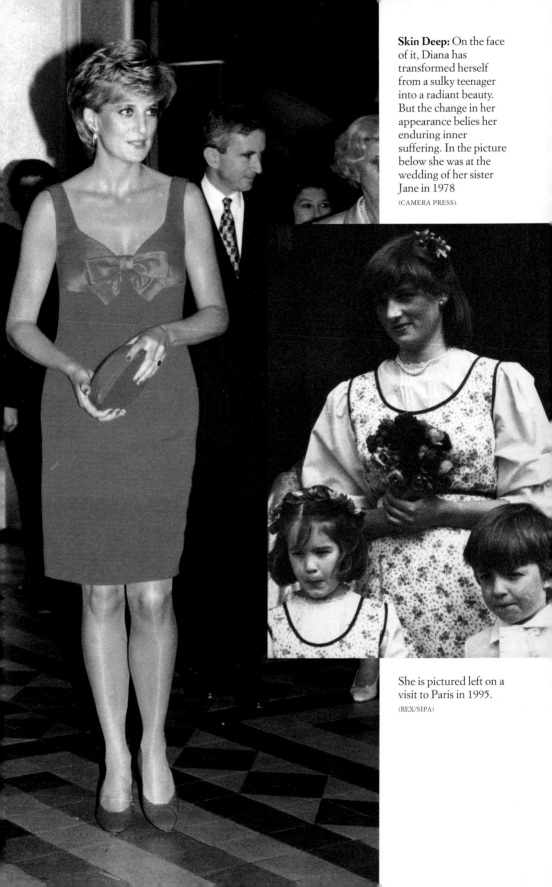

Skin Deep: On the face of it, Diana has transformed herself from a sulky teenager into a radiant beauty. But the change in her appearance belies her enduring inner suffering. In the picture below she was at the wedding of her sister Jane in 1978 (CAMERA PRESS).

She is pictured left on a visit to Paris in 1995. (REX/SIPA)

Marriage of Inconvenience (above): Even as a radiant bride on the steps of St Paul's, Diana failed to hold the attention of her husband. According to Lord Archer, he was 'more interested in his gloves than the beautiful woman on his arm'. (ALPHA)

Belted Earl (right): Diana's father, Johnnie Spencer, was a difficult man, whose behaviour drove away his first wife.
(Terry Spencer, CAMERA PRESS)

Motherly Love (above):
A rare shot of Diana
with her mother,
Frances Shand Kydd,
who left home when she
was just six years old.
The picture was taken
at the wedding of
Diana's younger
brother Charles, a
marriage that has since
failed.

(G. Dalla Pozza, CAMERAPRESS)

Thin Times (left):
Diana was not the only
woman with an eating
disorder to be courted
by Charles. Her eldest
sister, Sarah, then
anorexic, went out with
him for over a year.

(John Scott, Camera Press)

Growing Apart
(above): After years
of keeping up
appearances, Diana was
unable to hide the way
she felt about her
husband as they toured
South Korea shortly
before the
announcement of their
separation in 1992.
(CAMERA PRESS)

Widening Gulf (above):
At a parade to mark the
Allies' victory in the
Gulf War, Charles and
Diana – then in a state
of armed neutrality –
showed not a glimmer
of celebration.
(STEWART MARK, CAMERAPRESS)

Bathing Beauty
(opposite): The woman
who, in the words of her
close friend, James
Gilbey, can 'sniff a
camera at a thousand
yards' performed for
the photographers on
a Caribbean beach.
(REX FEATURES)

Diplomatic Impunity (above): Elder statesman Henry Kissinger fell under Diana's spell at a charity dinner in New York. He had no qualms about being photographed glancing at her cleavage.
(DAVE CHANCELLOR, ALPHA)

War Paint (right): A heavily made up Diana in a scene from her notorious *Panorama* interview.
(REX FEATURES)

Brave Front (opposite): On the night Charles told the nation that he had cheated on her, Diana put on her most provocative dress and went to a party.
(CAMERA PRESS)

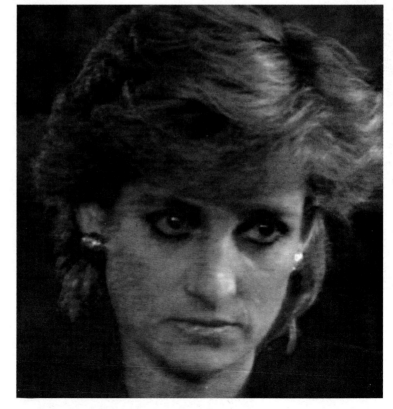

Going Native: Diana dons a *shalwar rhameez* on a visit to Imran Khan and his new wife, Jemima Goldsmith, in Lahore. (ALPHA)

Theatregoer (right): Diana's visit to Harefield Hospital to watch open-heart surgery proved a public-relations disaster as the TV pictures showed her in full make up and with her hair on display. (REX FEATURES)

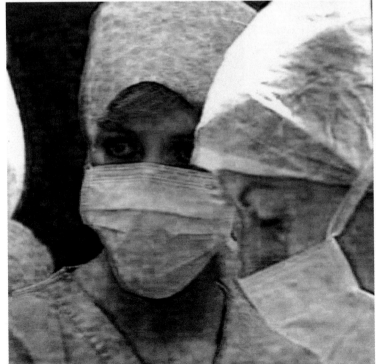

With hindsight she would have realized that elements of his behaviour were related to the pressures of his conflict. This could range from the extent to which he took an interest in her sexually to a general deterioration – or even improvement – in the quality of their relationship. In this way she and Diana were communicating, despite the fact they had never met, and the bitterness she feels towards Diana today is not just related to the fact of the Princess and her husband's close friendship but also to the resulting changes in him. He would have acted differently around the house. While Julia may have thought he appeared uncharacteristically vague as he sat in front of the television, he may have been thinking, as one expert colourfully put it to us of 'Diana as a tigress in bed'.

Diana, of course, had experienced related, but more far-reaching signs in her husband. She said on *Panorama* it was a 'woman's instinct' that told her that her husband had resumed his affair with Mrs Parker Bowles. Asked exactly how she could tell, she replied, 'By the change of behavioural pattern in my husband, for all sorts of reasons that a woman's instinct produces, you just know. It was already difficult, but it became increasingly difficult.'

So what would Diana have been thinking when she was with Will Carling? 'Somewhere in her unconscious she would be feeling quite pleased really that Julia Carling was being put out by this,' says Dr Friedman. ' "Serves her right", she'd have thought.'

Diana's thoughts, however, were by no means exclusively focused on Mrs Carling. By this time she had developed even more of an interest in the fortunes of Tiggy Legge-Bourke. Diana insisted that she melt into the background when press photographs were taken of the family, and she banned her from the Princes' car. On one memorable occasion she reportedly went so far as to stop the royal convoy to have Legge-Bourke removed from their side and placed in a car full of security men. According to the *Mail on Sunday* she said: 'That girl is not family, she's just a servant.'

Her determination to limit Legge-Bourke's influence led to a bizarrely detailed list of instructions, the paper reported. 'Miss Legge-Bourke will not spend unnecessary time in the children's rooms,' she ordered. 'She may not read to them at night, nor supervise their bathtime or bedtime. She is to carry out a secretarial role in the arrangement of their time with their father, that is all.'

Rules surrounding her telephone calls to her sons became comically elaborate. 'William and Harry are to be taken to a lodge on the Sandringham estate in order to speak to me privately on the telephone during their stay. No one else, no staff or servants, is to be present during our conversations.' These apparent efforts to turn her children against their nanny and, by extension, their father had echoes of her own experience following her parents' break-up. Diana seemed condemned, in psychological terms, to act out what she did not understand.

Ultimately it all proved counter-productive. So unreasonable were her demands that they began to be ignored altogether, and she soon lost any authority over Legge-Bourke she might ever have had. She even signally failed to turn her children against their nanny. William and Harry adored the lively and playful Tiggy-in-the-middle. Nothing could have incensed Diana more than Legge-Bourke's visit to Eton to visit William. The pair were photographed strolling across the playing fields with the Prince's pet labrador, Widgeon, and it was obvious that a close and relaxed relationship had been formed between them.

Diana's growing conviction that she had been usurped as a mother was soon joined by the notion that Legge-Bourke might also replace her as a wife. She made increasingly determined efforts to establish the nature of the relationship between Prince Charles and the nanny, monitoring their every move, poring over newspaper photographs of them embracing for any sign of unseemly intimacy. Her suspicions grew, and she eventually concluded that they must be having an affair. The incident at the Lanesborough Hotel was the culmination of this train of thought. But Dr Crown views Diana's remark there about not enjoying sex with Charles as more significant than the sarcastic barb that preceded it. He sees it as an issue the couple had perhaps failed to resolve.

'I would think Charles was probably incompetent, and she was inexperienced,' he says. 'With sexual problems, which is one of my special areas of involvement, it's always important to remember that it's fifty-fifty until it's proved otherwise, which it almost never is. In matters of sexuality there are no heroes and heroines, or double-dyed villains. They both got pushed into this marriage by forces that the ordinary person just can't envisage. People would have said to him, "This is the right thing to do and the right time. You're getting a bit old now. For God's sake get married," and so on. And she was around.

'I would have thought that the remark, "I hope you enjoyed it [sex with Charles] because I never did," absolutely expresses what I would say. Sexual problems take every form, from the fact that people can't communicate on a verbal level to issues of sexual technique. When you're dealing with sexual problems you've got to be very specific about things. Exactly where does it go wrong? Somewhere in the enormously long sequence: starting with communication, starting with fondling, starting with arousal, coming to erection and orgasm and the timing of all that. The problem could be anywhere. You can't guess at that.'

In general Diana's treatment of those she sees as a threat to her relationship with her sons or her husband, or to her standing in public life, is with a greater or lesser degree of hostility. Nowhere is her increasingly erratic conduct more marked than in her dealings with her rivals. It is the sort of behaviour that is beginning to alienate the neutrals in her conflict with Charles and the Royal Family. Never has she had a greater need for friends.

FIVE

ABSENT
FRIENDS

'Her social world has fallen to pieces, and
that is a big danger.'

Dr Sidney Crown, psychiatrist and consultant at the Royal London Hospital

When newsagent heiress Kate Menzies married chi-chi restau-
rateur Simon Slater in February 1996, it was one of the
society weddings of the year. But one person who was not present –
and whose absence dominated coverage of the event – was the
Princess of Wales. On her girlfriend's big day Diana was almost
4000 miles away in Lahore, visiting the cancer hospital run by the
former Pakistan cricket captain, Imran Khan, newly married to
Jemima Goldsmith.

Diana has grown to depend on the wise counsel of Lady
Annabel Goldsmith, mother of Jemima and husband of the pluto-
cratic Sir James, and has always been drawn to the sick and
underprivileged, wherever they may be, but to accept an invitation
on the wedding day of a woman who was considered one of her
closest friends appeared to some as a calculated snub.

Menzies had become especially close to Diana since being introduced to her by the Princess's sister-in-law Sarah, Duchess of York,
known to the world as Fergie. Such was Diana's trust in her new
friend's judgement that she soon allowed her to take over the
Duchess's job of finding suitable dinner parties for her to attend and

61

– more sensitively – discreet escorts to accompany her. But relations had cooled by the time of Menzies' nuptials.

The trail had been laid the previous winter, when, during a holiday in the Austrian skiing resort of Lech, Diana rowed with Kate Menzies and was heard to shout after her, following one exchange, 'I can't believe you said that!' And those six words carried a significance that belied their spontaneity. Diana, her marriage in ruins, her prospects of becoming Queen long dashed and with a string of therapists emphasizing the importance of being 'strong', was not prepared to stand for the overfamiliarity of her Sloaney set any longer.

From that moment Menzies' days as a member of her inner circle were numbered. And when her friend's engagement went through a rocky patch, Diana, in typically self-obsessed mood, said she had too many problems of her own to nurse anyone else through theirs. We can only assume what happened next, but, if their relationship took the course that so many others had, we have a good idea. In what has become a familiar pattern, those about to be summarily dumped find their calls are not returned, invitations dry up, and Diana's characteristic volubility is replaced by mono-syllabic responses. Rarely are any charges of misconduct made satisfactorily clear, and there is absolutely no right of appeal.

The list of ex-friends is extensive. Former flatmate Carolyn Bartholomew and Lady Stevens, wife of Lord Stevens of Ludgate, chairman of United Newspapers, are both reported to have lost touch. Major David Waterhouse and old Etonian Philip Dunne, enlisted to keep Diana company during a skiing holiday with Charles in the early days of their marriage, are very much old chums these days. And Catherine Soames, ex-wife of Diana's tormentor-in-chief Nicholas Soames, sees increasingly little of her. Those who have remained royal confidantes are Hyatt Palumbo, wife of property tycoon Lord Palumbo, who defected from the Charles camp, and Lady Gillian Rees-Mogg, wife of the former *Times* editor William Rees-Mogg.

Julia Samuel, who used to make up threesomes to the cinema with Diana and Major Waterhouse, is still on Diana's Christmas card list, but her cause cannot be helped by the fact she is the sister of Sabrina Guinness, the society beauty who had a passionate fling with Prince Charles in 1979. Another who remains in contact with Diana is the Honourable Rosa Monckton, wife of Dominic Lawson, editor of the *Sunday Telegraph*. Diana is godmother to their daughter Domenica, and the two women have spent holidays together. It was Monckton, the Roman Catholic managing director of Tiffany's the jewellers, who introduced her to Father Anthony Sutch at a dinner party in Belgravia, after which the Benedictine monk declared: 'The Princess was looking for an answer.'

One royal writer has attributed these amendments to the royal address book to a social shift away from the titled set to 'a more broadly based and meritocratic circle'. She is said to be close to showbiz names such as comedienne Ruby Wax and television presenter Clive James, for example. But, whatever lies behind this changing of the social guard, the rapid turnover means that very few of Diana's intimates date back more than two or three years. Psychiatrist Dr Dennis Friedman attributes this to her impossibly high expectations of her intimates. 'I think she is constantly looking for somebody or something that will make her feel better,' he says, 'and it sounds very much as if every time she finds a new friend she thinks, This is it, if it's a new man. He's going to love me, or She will understand me, or She will be my bosom friend, because her bosom friend disappeared soon after she was born. She has expectations that are never fulfilled, and because of the self-fulfilling prophecy, she sets up situations in which they can't be.'

Fellow psychiatrist Dr Sidney Crown puts it even more power-fully. He says, 'Her social world has fallen to pieces' and describes this as a 'worrying' trend. 'I think she is the sort of person who, even if she wasn't in the sort of position she is, would find it quite difficult to maintain her friends because she's very self-centred. She's a very narcissistic person. I think she would probably find it very difficult to give very much. And there's a limit to the extent to which friends will tolerate self-centredness. I understand if you get her on the telephone you can never get her off it, but she's always talking about herself.

'Most people have a limit . . . they can't just be sucked dry all the time, and I would guess, with Diana, that she makes such demands on people that even those who are closest to her find that they simply can't cope with that any more. And when they show that in some way, she then has to get rid of them.

'Now, what has come on top of that is, because of her position, she's actually vulnerable, and she's not a very good judge of people. She's understandably very suspicious of the people around her. I mean, I was at a meeting of doctors last night where we were talking about BSE, and I had this sort of feeling: I wonder if that's a *Mirror* reporter who's crept in. You get quite suspicious of people in that situation. So, therefore, I would think that she is now limited to those who are harmless, often youngsters, because a lot of lonely people have got excellent relationships with kids because of their spontaneity.

'So I think that, yes, her social world has fallen to pieces, and that is a big danger. I think that she is in tremendous confusion by not having any support from friends, because she can't give to them, they can't give to her, and she's suspicious of them.'

Dr Crown describes this feature of her social relations as 'very striking' and reckons it is at the root of her visits to various therapists. 'It's fair to say that everyone has problems in their life, but the vast majority of people sort it out by themselves, with their partner or with their friends,' he says. 'They don't need professional help. Women develop very meaningful, close and lasting relationships with each other – not of a sexual sort, I'm not talking about that – but of a supportive sort. But Diana builds up relationships, same-sex relationships, then dumps them just as she does with opposite-sex relationships. It's very self-destructive and has left her a very lonely figure with no one to turn to.

'Friends are so important. I'm constantly struck with what helpful and deep-seated relationships women make with women. Without the sexual implications that come with opposite-sex relations, they feel they can be very open with each other. She's got rid of women as quickly as she's got rid of men. I think she probably does have difficulty with commitment. If one has to guess about that psychologically, then I would concentrate on her pretty unhappy background, because that's where the ability to commit starts: when you are tiny, and your mother can pat you and cuddle you, talk to you, breast-feed you and so on.

'My daughter's just had a baby, and, watching it all over again, it's quite interesting to see how the bonding builds up. People who bond well when they are small, not only bond better later on but, the paradox is, they can also be separate much more effectively. If that isn't done, if there is never any adequate reward in the system the person's brought up in – any affection, tenderness, love, those sort of things, and it does sound very much as if she hasn't had that – it makes it extremely difficult for people to build up trusting relationships, friendships with anybody afterwards. So if I was seeing her as a patient I would move into that area.'

Susan Quilliam describes Diana as a 'man's woman' and, like Dr Crown, traces the development of this characteristic to her mother's departure. 'A child who is faced with a withdrawn parent will do absolutely everything, move heaven and earth, to get that parent's attention,' she says, 'often to the extent that the other loving parent – in this case her mother – thinks, What am I doing this for? I give her everything, and it's her dad she's trying to get attention from. So my guess is that any trouble started well before Diana was six. The traditional age is a year, 18 months, where mum's already saying, "She's a daddy's girl, she whinges with me all day, but she's all smiles for daddy in the evening."

'And in that situation, having tried to get daddy's attention, mummy may walk out. OK, in some respects, that's great because the little girl has now got daddy to herself; but when she loses mum, she loses all the stability. She loses her role model, and she still hasn't got daddy. Daddy is trying to get over the broken marriage, he sends her away to school, and then he turns round and marries somebody else. So now we've got a pattern that could go either way. Diana could have become a man-hater, but it's turned out differently. I cannot say whether or not, when that happens to a child, they will become a man's woman. What I can say is that being a man's woman comes from a number of roots, and this is one of them.'

Diana cannot even rely on the support of all members of her immediate family. Her sister Jane's marriage to the Queen's private secretary, Sir Robert Fellowes, puts both of them in an invidious position. Diana came to see her brother-in-law as public enemy number one, identifying him as the unseen hand behind many of her misfortunes. Throughout Diana's increasingly public spats with Jane's husband and his office, however the sisters had managed to maintain a sound friendship.

Jane had always been the conformist. Something of an academic by Spencer family standards, she actually gained some O and A levels and had even been captain of the lacrosse team and a sixth-form prefect. To this day she is an active member of the Old Girls' Association. Unlike her younger sister she avoids shopping binges at Harvey Nichols and celebrity spots such as San Lorenzo, preferring evenings at home with her husband. But it took the *Panorama* interview to drive a wedge between them. There was an extended row – on the telephone, naturally – as Diana demanded her sister's support, only to be told she was supporting her husband of 17 years, who had found the whole exercise a betrayal of mammoth proportions.

The course of sisterly affection runs more smoothly between Diana and her eldest sibling, Sarah, now Lady Sarah McCorquodale, following her wedding to Neil McCorquodale in May 1980 on the Spencer family's Althorp Estate, at which Diana was chief bridesmaid. She joined Diana's alternative court as a lady-in-waiting after the split with Prince Charles, and the pair have remained close ever since. Diana has a more ambivalent relationship with her only brother, Charles, who inherited the Spencer earldom in 1992. He was one of the prime movers behind the organization of Andrew Morton's sympathetic biography of his sister, but his unconditional support has ebbed since. In April 1993 he offered Diana a house on the family estate, but within three weeks he had retracted the offer, citing the nuisance of extra police and surveillance cameras.

The temperature of the relationship between Diana and her stepmother, Raine, meanwhile, has rarely risen above freezing. Dr Crown even suggests that by marrying Raine, Countess of Dartmouth, a woman to whom Diana had a deep and abiding antipathy, her father effectively became the first man to reject her. 'Yes, not only the first but, in a sense, the most important,' he argues. 'That would be a very strong explanation of why she finds such difficulty in building up relationships and committing to relationships now. It is a very clear pattern.'

His analysis is shared by Susan Quilliam. 'Most bonding to one gender – because there are women who get on much better with women than they do with men – is to do with something that's happened in early childhood. In some cases the daughter is very strongly bonded to her father and therefore can't get on with women. In others she's very weakly bonded and spent all her childhood trying to seek her father's attention, and therefore, when she grows up, she hasn't got time for women, because she's still too busy trying to get men's attention That's certainly what happened with Diana. My guess is the problem started before her mother walked out.'

Surprisingly enough, one of the most enduring of Diana's confidantes has been her erstwhile sister-in-law, the Duchess of York. It was Diana who smoothed Sarah Ferguson's passage into the Royal Family by inviting her to dinner at Windsor Castle and fostering her subsequent relationship with Prince Andrew. But, since then, their friendship has narrowly survived a series of ructions.

Diana first began to distance herself from the Duchess of York after some ill-advised high jinks in the Royal Enclosure at Ascot, which involved prodding a succession of racegoers on the bottom with furled umbrellas. Diana was mortified by the publicity that followed and resolved to distance herself from her sister-in-law thereafter.

By late 1989 good relations had been partially restored. The Duchess was, however, kept at arm's length until some time after that disastrous day in August 1992, when she and Diana, along with the rest of the Royal Family gathered at Balmoral, were devastated by the newspaper publication of photographs showing her topless beside a pool in the south of France with Johnny Bryan kissing her toes in full view of the princesses Beatrice and Eugenie. Sarah was banished from the castle in disgrace, and all calls to her sister-in-law went unreturned.

Things took a different turn later that year on the morning of Sunday, 6 December, when, to her surprise, Diana called her from Kensington Palace. When she heard the words, 'Hello, Duch, this is Squidgy,' Sarah knew Diana was in conciliatory mood. In the 30-minute conversation that followed it became clear that their relationship was back on track. Diana even told her sister-in-law – three days before the Prime Minister announced it in the Commons – that a separation from Charles was imminent and that she had already moved all her things out of Highgrove.

In late 1995 they began lunching together every Sunday at the

Duchess's Surrey home. It is a measure of Diana's desperation that she was forced to turn to Sarah as a soul mate. Time may have dulled public recollection of the humiliating toe-sucking pictures, but the Duchess's reputation continued to take a battering. The stream of damaging revelations seemed endless: her debts were spiralling out of control, she was becoming obsessed with money-making deals, she was pursuing a handsome young tennis star.

In such circumstances it is clear why the Duchess of York would be interested in cultivating relations with her less tarnished sister-in-law. As Gilbey so insightfully observed to Diana during their taped conversation: 'All I worry about . . . you know, that she's desperate, darling, she's desperately trying to get back in. She's trying to tag on, because she knows your PR is so good. So she's trying to tack on to it.'

Dr Crown argues that little good can come of the relationship. 'It is a very complicated thing between the two of them in the sense that neither is particularly bright or educated, and their personalities are very similar,' he argues. 'They are both exceptionally narcissistic. A patient of mine who works in these circles told me she happened to be on holiday a year ago in the entourage around Fergie in some Swiss village, and Fergie decided she wanted to go shopping at five o'clock on a Sunday afternoon. Everything was shut, and they had to open up for her. What I'm really saying is that Fergie and Diana would be swimming in a sea of narcissism.

'I can quite imagine that they take it in turns to pour out their hearts over various things. They wouldn't interact really, and they wouldn't actually listen very much to what the other is saying. They would talk at each other, and they both have a feeling that nobody rates them highly enough. Diana feels she's not rated highly enough for her Mother Teresa and other activities. Fergie's denigrated because of her spendthrift ways. But they just talk like that, and so, in a sense, I would think that the relationship is the worst possible thing for both of them.'

As the Duchess's money worries mounted – she was said to owe £3 million before her divorce in May 1996 – she was certainly in no position to offer Diana the sort of sound and reasoned advice she needed. The Princess's closest royal ally was prone to violent mood swings and had frequent tearful altercations with her staff. She turned to a bizarre assortment of fortune-tellers, astrologers and alternative therapists to advise her on how to act. Her call to fortune-teller Rita Rogers became the most important single event in her day, and she was often heard to declare that she was becoming 'more spiritual by the minute'.

Diana's healthiest relationships appear to be with older women. For a long time her mother figure was Lucia Flecha de Lima, 55, the wife of the then Brazilian ambassador to London, whom she met on an official visit to Brazil in 1991. With her own mother living in rural isolation on the Isle of Seil off the west coast of Scotland, Diana adopted a woman whose own children had grown up and who had time to nurture her. Mrs Flecha de Lima was just the sort of wise old bird that Diana needed. The eldest of nine children of a wealthy heiress and a professor of tropical medicine, she had grown up in some style in a 44-room neo-classical *Gone With the Wind*-style house with a staff to match. Happily married since her teens, her stable influence saw Diana through some of her most difficult crises.

Their friendship followed the familiar, rather one-sided, pattern. Diana would call at all hours of the day or night, wrenching the kindly Mrs Flecha de Lima from dinner parties or dragging her out of bed for a therapeutic chat. Entire weekends would be spent at the ambassadorial residence on Mount Street in Mayfair, where Diana could kick off her shoes and sample the sort of informal family life that had been denied her as a child.

Mrs Flecha de Lima, in alliance with Lady Palumbo, also encouraged Diana to make forays into the outside world. On one occasion the trio even hired a small plane to cross the Channel to Le Bourget, completing the journey to Paris in the most unroyal of vehicles, a minibus. In the French capital they spent two days in an orgy of shopping and lunching. There was even a lobster dinner with French actor Gerard Depardieu and a date at the Ritz with *Schindler's List* director Steven Spielberg. Other trips were made to Bali and the Indian Ocean island of Moyo. It was a dark day, therefore, when Lucia's husband, Paolo-Tarso, was named the new ambassador to Washington. On hearing the news, the devastated Princess fled a theatre in tears and rushed round to see her friend. And on the day the Flecha de Limas flew out, she was at the airport to say her farewells.

Since then her role has been taken on by Lady Annabel Goldsmith, now said to be among Diana's most trusted confidantes. Other members of the group unkindly dubbed Matrons Anonymous are Angela Serota, the estranged wife of the director of the Tate Gallery, psychotherapist Susie Orbach, and Baroness Jay, who defended her stoutly against Charles's man, Nicholas Soames, in the *Newsnight* debate that followed her *Panorama* interview.

Psychologist Susan Quilliam attributes this quest for mature support to the destabilizing effect of being thrust into the limelight at a vulnerable age. 'Diana's not had a normal life,' she says. 'From the time she was 19 she's been thrown from pillar to post, or she sent herself from pillar to post, so she's liable to have been through a lot of emotional changes, and she may be at the stage where she just doesn't want people of her own age. She wants mother figures.'

'One's got to remember,' says Dr Crown, 'that every relationship we build up with somebody who means a lot to us has all sorts of components to it. I keep saying this because I don't want anyone to think that we're making her unique. Where you have somebody who's had a very [emotionally] deprived childhood, with both mother and father letting her down very badly, she'll always be looking for substitutes. To some extent Charles is a father figure. The age gap between them is significantly bigger than the average, which tends to be four or five years. I would say she almost certainly has been looking for parental substitutes, and that's why she does make better relationships with older women, particularly one who, in Orbach's case, is professionally bound not to let her down. I think she feels there is solidity there.'

The extent of her neediness is exposed in the Squidgygate tape, so called after James Gilbey's term of endearment. He calls Diana 'darling' 53 times and 'Squidgy' or 'Squidge' 14 times. At one point he says to her, 'You don't mind it, darling, when I want to talk to you so much?'; to which she replies poignantly, 'No, I love it. Never had it before, I've never had it before.' He responds with: 'Darling, it's so nice being able to help you'; and this evokes even more heartfelt gratitude: 'You do . . . you'll never know how much. You'll never know how much.'

At this stage Gilbey was obviously well tutored in the arts of consoling unhappy princesses. There are a series of almost pantomime displays of affection. He says, 'Kiss me, darling,' and she blows a kiss. Then he promises to keep his mobile phone about him rather than leave it in the car, so she can contact him at any time, before admitting: 'You know, darling, I could not sort of face the thought of not speaking to you every free moment. Fills me with real horror, you know.'

Gilbey's friendship with Diana appears to be one of her most enduring. The pair first met before her marriage when he was working for a car-rental company in Victoria, and they had a series of dates. On one famous occasion Gilbey had the temerity to stand her up. It was not a mistake he would ever repeat. Knowing how fond he was of his sporty Alfa Romeo, the petulant teenager showed an early talent for going for the jugular. With great conscientiousness, she and a friend mixed a bucketful of flour, eggs and water and, under cover of darkness, poured it over his beloved motor. By morning it had set to form a rock-solid reminder that she was not a woman with whom to be trifled.

Despite these inauspicious beginnings they kept in contact, and, while her denial of adultery with him on *Panorama* is perfectly credible, it was clear that they were still on affectionate terms. 'I felt very protective about James,' she said, 'because he'd been a very good friend to me and was a very good friend to me, and I couldn't bear that his life was going to messed up because he had the connection with me. And that worried me. I'm very protective about my friends.'

Unfortunately for Diana not everyone shared Gilbey's admiration of her and her works. Complaining about how the rest of the Royal Family were keeping a distance from her, during her conversation with Gilbey she said: 'The distancing will be because I go out and – I hate the word – conquer the world. I don't mean that. I mean, I will go and and do my own bit in the way I know how.' She goes on: 'I had a very bad lunch, I nearly started blubbering. I just felt really sad over lunch. I thought, Bloody hell, what I've done for this f*****g family.'

Dr Crown reckons part of her difficulty in maintaining relationships with friends may lie in the tremendous power that her popularity breeds and the fawning acolytes it attracts. 'If you think of the megalomaniac dictators of today,' he says, 'the extreme example being the Husseins and the Hitlers, power has totally consumed them, and there's nobody around who can stop that. Now, with the ordinary person who becomes powerful – a powerful businessman, for instance – there are people around them who can keep their psychological feet on the ground.

'The danger with Diana is that if she combines her great power, her great charisma, with isolation, it could be very dangerous. I don't think it would lead her to break down, but it could make her an even more impossible person, totally self-centred, and people dislike that sort of thing. Nobody likes somebody who is totally self-important.'

There was no greater evidence of Diana's isolation than on the May bank holiday weekend in 1996 when she was driven to Heathrow airport for an impulse trip abroad. First she joined the queue of passengers at the Iberia check-in for the flight to Alicante. Then she and a middle-aged female friend, Susie Kassem, an interior designer, headed for the Bureau de Change to buy pesos. By now the photographers who kept a round-the-clock vigil in the departure lounge on the look-out for travelling celebrities had spotted her. While Diana remonstrated with them, her friend said of the ticket they had just bought: 'It's not for her, it's for me. I'm very sick, I'm very ill, and I need help.' Then the pair took refuge in the ladies' lavatories for 15 minutes. Finally, using the ticket that was allegedly 'not for her', Diana boarded the plane and set off for Spain.

On arrival at Alicante she hailed an airport cab and told the driver to find her 'a nice hotel'. At the Sidi San Juan tourist hotel close to Benidorm, a resort better known for its lager louts than its champagne Charlies, she was then forced to plead for a room after initially being told there was none available. She spent 18 hours alone in her room, before informing the manager that she would not be staying three nights after all and promptly returned to the airport to fly home to London. When approached by fellow passengers in the first-class cabin, she blanked them all. It was obviously not one of her days for being Queen of people's hearts.

It was subsequently claimed by Diana's press spokeswoman, Jane Atkinson, that she had made the trip to visit a sick friend, but there was nothing to back this up. On the contrary it began to look as if, friendless and alone on a holiday weekend, she had made a spontaneous and ill-judged decision to fly somewhere hot.

The diameter of her social circle will not be helped by her divorce, which represents the severing of a key link with the Royal Family. One who married into royal circles herself, Lady Colin Campbell, author of *Diana in Private* and *The Royal Marriages*, reckons that, despite Diana's evergreen appeal to the general public, parts of high society began to drop her 'like hot cakes' as soon as the separation was announced.

'A lot of Establishment people, a lot of the duchesses, the sort of people who would normally be happy to have her along, crossed her off their lists,' she says. 'When her name was brought up, people said, "Oh, no, no, no. We wouldn't dream of asking her, she's behaved badly," or else they didn't want to antagonize Buckingham Palace by asking her, so they'd ask someone else, who was less glamorous but more worthy in royal terms, someone like the Duchess of Kent.'

Diana felt the effects of this ostracization on a more everyday level too. 'I would imagine that quite a number of her friends just wouldn't want to be drawn into the whole business,' says Dr Dorothy Rowe. 'You know what it's like when you discover that a couple you're friendly with are going through the process of divorce, and you have to make a decision about whether you're going to stay close to them or move away. And if you are going to stay close to them, you usually end up having to decide which one of them. So an awful lot of friendships dissolve when divorces come through.'

With her inner circle so whittled down, with so few friends left in whom Diana felt able to confide, it is, perhaps, little wonder that she needed to invest so much faith in a psychotherapist from north London, Susie Orbach.

SIX

THE ORBACH INFLUENCE

'I know that every therapist has pondered having Diana as a client.'

DR DOROTHY ROWE, CLINICAL PSYCHOLOGIST

By spring 1996 politicians were calling Diana the pink princess. While Prime Minister John Major vacillated over her future role in public life, Opposition leader Tony Blair seized the political initiative to praise her in the wake of her *Panorama* interview. She, in return, described him as 'charismatic' at a lunch with *Guardian* journalists.

Recognizing the grim prospect of the Princess's awesome popularity being exploited by New Labour during a General Election campaign, Conservative politicians were quick to identify her therapist, Susie Orbach, as the doctrinaire influence behind Diana's sudden interest in politics. The daughter of the late Maurice Orbach, a Labour MP, Orbach has made no secret of her socialist leanings. In her book *Hunger Strike* she wrote: 'For women, the culture of greed exemplified by Reagan's America and Thatcher's Britain was both beckoning and forbidding, tempting and denying.'

She appeared to have passed on some of her fervour for the cause to her most celebrated client. And there was more to the mutual back-slapping between Diana and the forces of the radical centre than an exchange of compliments with Blair. Breaking all the royal rules about staying above politics, Diana had also written a letter to a left-wing Labour MP endorsing his attack on government policy towards welfare claimants.

This followed close behind the political storm prompted by her appearance alongside Jack Straw, Labour's shadow Home Secretary, at an event organized by the homeless charity Centrepoint. Taking her sons to a homeless shelter in the Soho area of London was also interpreted as a move to show the Princes that the hard-done-by suffered more under the Tories. Even her choice of divorce lawyers, Mishcon de Reya, a firm founded by the socialist peer Lord Mishcon, was seen as evidence of her love-in with New Labour.

Since Diana had first heard Orbach speak at a conference on eating disorders in April 1993 the two women had formed a powerful bond. By this time Orbach was a world authority on anorexia nervosa and bulimia nervosa, having followed up the success of her bestselling *Fat Is a Feminist Issue* with *Hunger Strike*, described by the *Times Literary Supplement* as 'a much needed antidote to the unsympathetic views often aroused by anorexia nervosa'.

Apart from each being mothers of two and having a history of eating disorders, the women had very different lifestyles when Diana began seeing Orbach on a professional basis in the wake of Prince Charles's confession of his adultery in a television interview with Jonathan Dimbleby in 1994. Orbach was a commoner with republican sympathies, while Diana, as the daughter of an earl and a heartbeat from the monarchy, was a pillar of the Establishment. Orbach was short, small-framed and distinctly nervy, Diana was tall, muscular and introverted. The therapist was 49, her royal client 15 years younger.

But they soon developed a strong relationship. The confused Princess required her sympathetic ear and unique expertise. Orbach had no reason to regret her very public contact with the world's most famous basket-case (to use Diana's own terminology). As Orbach's friend Dr Dorothy Rowe says: 'I know that every therapist of whatever persuasion has pondered having Diana as a client, because there's tremendous competition now among therapists. It's a booming business, and there's only a certain amount of trade available, so you need to have some kind of cachet to your name.' And there can be no greater cachet than adding the Princess of Wales to your client list. Orbach duly found herself the most famous psychotherapist in Britain, complete with her own TV series.

Orbach's influence on her royal patient is undeniably huge. As Diana's psychotherapist, she has been credited with encouraging a spate of outspoken comments, including the *Panorama* interview itself. Orbach told her to speak her mind and not bottle up her emotions, and her then private secretary, Patrick Jephson, was said to have felt undermined by the therapist's growing influence. A friend of his said that since Diana had been seeing Orbach: 'She has changed radically – *Panorama* was the manifestation of the new Diana.'

Most patients go through what is known as a 'transference' phase with a therapist, this is the term used to describe the period during the relationship when a client develops an emotional attitude, positive or negative, towards their therapist or becomes particularly dependent on them.

Orbach was certainly available to Diana at short notice. It was to her the Princess turned on Boxing Day 1995, after enduring the most dispiriting Christmas of her life. Cut off from her sons by her decision not to join the rest of the Royal Family at Sandringham, she had spent Christmas Day alone in her apartment, with only a skeleton staff on duty. Diana pulled up outside her therapist's brick and stucco house on a tree-lined road in up-market Belsize Park soon after lunch. They climbed the stairs to the sparsely furnished, top-floor room where all their £70 sessions are held, and Diana took her customary seat on a sofa, with Orbach in an easy chair close by.

Their discussions took place a stone's throw from the place where Sigmund Freud, the father of psychoanalysis and the man who set the pattern for Orbach's approach, settled in the thirties. He placed great reliance on taking his patients back to childhood traumas in the belief that, by analysing and confronting them anew, they would recover through the resulting 'catharsis'. This was very fertile ground in Diana's case. For all the privilege she was born into, she had experienced an emotionally turbulent childhood. She was just six when her mother earned the nickname 'the bolter' by walking out on the family for another man.

'My parents were busy sorting themselves out,' Diana once revealed. 'I remember my mother crying, daddy never spoke to us about it. We could never ask questions. Too many nannies. The whole thing was very unstable.'

Orbach coaxed out of her the tales of persecution at the hands of some of her nannies, the emotional tug-of-war between her parents and her schooldays bulimia that are outlined in chapter 10. It was the bulimia that persisted into her adult life, and it is this condition that fell into Orbach's special area of competence.

But while Orbach may have become her principal adviser, Diana was not about to abandon her visits to the various alternative therapists she had consulted from time to time over the preceding years. With 40,000 people in Britain alone earning a living from practising talking cures, she was spoilt for choice. Such is the popularity of these more fringe therapies that practising astrologers even outnumber clinical psychologists in Britain. If sociology were the discipline that dominated thinking in the seventies and early eighties, psychology and its New Age relations hold sway in popular thinking today.

Diana was certainly impressed by its messages, and she leaves little to chance in her tour of the capital's most exclusive private practitioners. Her possibly stress-related back pain is treated by osteopath Michael Skipwith, the man who introduced her to Orbach. He uses rhythmic stretching and pressure to relieve tension in her back for £35 a session. This is complemented by a weekly 90-minute massage with essential oils from down-to-earth Yorkshire woman Sue Beechey, the aromatherapist she has been seeing for more than nine years. Diana also receives regular visits from Oonagh Toffolo, an Irish nurse from County Sligo, who specializes in dietary disorders, stress regulation and muscular tension. She called herself an acupuncturist but was not registered with any of the relevant major British acupuncture associations.

Diana is also a devotee of colonic irrigation, a procedure that will make many wince. It involves flushing warm purified water (or another liquid) through her intestine via a plastic pipe inserted in her rectum. Aficionados claim it is a highly effective way of clearing toxic waste products from the system or, as Diana puts it: 'It takes the aggro out of me.' Diana subjects herself to it once a fortnight, paying £60 an hour for the hydrotherapy treatment at the Hale Clinic near Regent's Park.

She is even reported to have enlisted the services of the Hale Clinic's Simone Simmons, an 'energy healer'. She apparently told Simmons that 'a negative entity' was giving her nightmares, disturbing her sleep by sitting on her chest. During a visit to the Princess's private rooms at Kensington Palace, Simmons traced the problem to 'a vast black whirlwind of energy' on the left side of Diana's double bed.

Indeed, on matters spiritual, Diana has left few stones unturned. Over the years she has consulted at least three astrologers – Penny Thornton, Felix Lyle and Debby Frank – and placed great store by the star charts they produced. In December 1988 she began consulting Stephen Twigg, a former junior tax inspector turned New Age thinker and masseur, who stressed the importance of linking health in mind and body, only terminating the relationship under Palace pressure after he gave an interview to Shirley Flack for the *Sunday Express* newspaper.

Diana has also consulted at least two psychics, Betty Palko and Rita Rogers. Both claim to have put her in touch with her dead father during seances. She met Irish clairvoyant Mrs Palko for Tarot card readings in discreet London hotels. Mrs Palko, who normally operated from a Tudor semi in Surbiton, claimed that Earl Spencer had appeared before her while the Princess was present and that she relayed messages between them.

On other occasions she would drive the 160 miles to a rambling Victorian house in a working-class suburb of Chesterfield to consult Rogers. Like Penny Thornton, Diana was introduced to this obscure provincial medium by her sister-in-law Sarah Ferguson. Rogers, who claims to specialize in contacting dead children, waives her £35-an-hour fee for the Princess. Rogers herself, who displays a Christmas card from her royal client on her coffee table, is keen to maintain her reputation for confidentiality.

'I meet an awful lot of celebrities and VIP people but I'm very, very discreet and very loyal to them,' she told the authors. 'I help people an awful lot with general guidance. I get people from

America and Africa, but I would never, never discuss none of them.' But down-to-earth Rogers is no respector of titles and obviously has yet to catch up with the elevation of the earl's daughter to princess. 'I'd have no comment to make on Lady Di or Sarah or anyone,' she adds. 'I would never discuss them with anybody and not just them. If it was Joe Bloggs from down the road I would not because I'm just a very loyal person.'

Quite how seriously Diana takes all this advice was illustrated by a remark she made during her Squidgygate conversation with James Gilby. She confessed to telling the Bishop of Norwich: 'I know this sounds a bit crazy, but I've lived before.'

Lady Colin Campbell attributes this tour of fringe therapy not to a spiritual attitude but to a very unspiritual one. 'If she had profound spirituality, she would understand the concept of responsibility,' she says. 'Ultimately each spiritual person regards their soul as the primary thing in life and believes in its enhancement in a good and constructive way, and thereafter the enhancement of other people's lives. She doesn't understand this, so she doesn't have the internal strength to appreciate the signals that life gives her, or that she gives herself or that other people give her. And so she seeks answers in crackpots.

'I wouldn't dream of going to a fortune-teller, and I don't think anyone who has a proper handle on spirituality should because then you are surrendering. You are letting in someone else on the bond between God and yourself. You are allowing someone else to determine your destiny and regulate your actions, your future, your effect upon other people. It's an abdication of spiritual responsibility.'

Dr Dorothy Rowe attributes Diana's suggestibility to her intellectual naivety. 'She hasn't had the kind of education that would teach her to be discriminating and to think in terms of probabilities and such, but then few people do have that education,' she says. 'If they did, astrologers would not be the rich people they are, and we wouldn't have astrology columns in virtually every national newspaper. We're not encouraged to let our children have an education that turns them into sceptics. You have to be a very sceptical person to be able to dismiss all that lot and see that you need to look for someone who's very hard-headed in terms of the search for what's actually going on.'

Dr Robert Lefever, on the other hand, sees them all as potentially disastrous distractions from the real issue. 'It's all part of trying to change something out there,' he argues. 'Something's wrong with people, places and things out there. We will look at anything except the compulsion. We will look at whether we've got the right hairstyle, whether we've got the right diet, whether we've got the right people looking after us, whether we've got the right whatever, anything rather than actually acknowledge that we are responsible for our own end. And anything that says we've got to learn to be more assertive and be our own selves is barking mad. We are the most arrogant, self-centred sods that ever existed. That's what addicts are. We believe in an old Alcoholics Anonymous saying, "It's I, I, I sung to the tune of me, me, me." Totally self-centred. That's what we need to lay aside, and say, "I'm just Joe Soap," and the capacity to do that is no more difficult for a princess than it is for a shopkeeper.'

More traditional therapists were taken less seriously, however. Most of the conventional treatment Diana has ever considered, she soon rejected as 'baffling'. When she was suffering from post-natal depression and bulimia in the early eighties after the birth of William, Prince Charles introduced her to Dr Allan McGlashlan, the elderly psychiatrist the Prince consults to this day. Dr McGlashlan is a disciple of the Swiss psychiatrist Carl Gustav Jung whose analytical psychology specialized in dream analysis. He encouraged her to provide written descriptions of her dreams, which he would then discuss with her. But she stopped seeing him soon after beginning the sessions.

Next came Dr David Mitchell. His method was to meet her every evening to listen to her version of the day's events. He was particularly interested in her accounts of her conversations with her husband, which he would then analyse. The sessions usually ended with the Princess in tears. Diana did not believe that Dr Mitchell was any closer to understanding her psyche than Dr McGlashlan.

In the light of this, and given that her post-natal depression was diagnosed by the royal gynaecologist Dr George Pinker, her

Panorama criticism of those close to her for not supporting her, is unjust. Conveniently forgetting Charles's efforts to retain the services of Dr McGlashlan and others, she complained: 'Maybe I was the first person ever to be in this family who ever had a depression or was ever openly tearful. And obviously that was daunting because if you've never seen it before, how do you support it?' Adding: 'It gave everybody a wonderful new label – Diana's unstable and Diana's mentally unbalanced. And, unfortunately, that seems to have stuck on and off over the years.'

Quite how long Susie Orbach can expect to retain her confidence is a matter of some conjecture. Some counsellors believe that Diana is too self-indulgent to cope well with any kind of Freudian approach, which demands a great deal of work on the part of the patient. They are expected to go on an emotional roller-coaster ride through their childhood traumas. Another problem is Diana's likely resentment of the BBC's exploitation of the fame she indirectly bestowed on Orbach. A source close to the Princess suggested Diana was reluctant to share her with a television audience, and when Orbach landed her own series, there were signs their professional relationship had peaked.

Psychotherapists' relationships with their clients can last for years, but any association with Diana is always vulnerable to an abrupt termination. Such a move would be no judgement on Orbach's professional abilities, says Dr Dennis Friedman. 'I think Susie Orbach is a very good therapist,' he says. 'I speak to her on the phone sometimes. She's well known in psychology. I'm not a psychologist, I'm a psychiatrist, but we did have a patient in common a year or so ago, and I think she's very good. She's written a lot, she's got a very good reputation, but I think that Diana is always looking for something new, something else. It wouldn't be a reflection on Susie Orbach if she did, it would be something to do with Diana's needs. She can't imagine that any one person could possibly help her.'

Dr Sidney Crown agrees: 'It's difficult to guess how long Diana and Susie Orbach will last because all we've heard so far is that when Diana gets comfortable in relationships, she breaks them up. Susie Orbach is extremely experienced and would anticipate that and would be constantly putting it to her: "You are wanting to get

out of this relationship just as you get out of all other relationships."
In other words she would make Diana look at it before she did it.
And so, therefore, it might well last.'

There have already been suggestions that Orbach has been
sharing her client with at least one psychiatrist. This would be a
damaging arrangement, according to Dr Crown. 'What you can't
usually do is to have more than one relatively conventional
therapist,' he says, 'and, although Susie Orbach is regarded by some
people as not being conventional, she actually is. I read an article
she wrote the other day, and it was very conventional Freudian stuff,
almost old-fashioned in fact. I think it would be very difficult for
her to work with Diana if she was seeing another conventional
therapist. You just get muddled messages, and Diana would suffer,
so you simply don't do that.

'If I were the psychiatrist, and Susie Orbach the therapist, I
would need to talk to Susie. It would then depend on how I got on
with her and how she got on with me. It might be possible to evolve
some way of working that wouldn't be damaging to the client, but
it's very difficult.

'The other point [in sharing a client] that makes it very difficult
is that part of the received wisdom of therapy is that the person the
client goes to first always has "the relationship". It's just the way we
human beings work, and so it's very difficult for anyone to be called
in at a later stage. Someone else can take over if the therapist is ill
or dying or something, but that's different, that's replacement. It
would be very difficult for someone else to get involved since she's
been going to Susie Orbach for so long.

'You might be able to make it work if you've got a different
approach. If someone needs drugs, for example, I say well, you go
to Dr X for that and come to me for the talking, but I wouldn't try
to overlap. You each have a separate role. Although it would be
difficult, Diana might do that because she tends to rush around in
circles to so many different helping services. That's why she might
try to do it, but whether they [the therapists] would go along with
it, I don't know. They certainly wouldn't do it if she were an
ordinary person.'

But not everyone has such high praise for Orbach. In a small flat
near London's Maudsley Hospital lives an octogenarian psychol-

ogist called Hans Eysenck. It was he who unsettled psychologists in 1950 when he published the results of research into the effect of psychoanalysis on patients. To the amazement of the academic and clinical communities his research supported the theory that patients on waiting lists at American hospitals who did not see psycho-analysts fared better than those who did.

'Analysing, if anything, makes the patient worse,' says Dr David Nias, a disciple of Eysenck, who has written a number of books with him. 'It makes them dwell on their problems in an effort to find reasons for it in their childhood so they can blame themselves and that sort of thing, which tends to be destructive. As I say, although that has been all the fashion, academically, it's totally debunked. What the immediate future is for the patient is all that matters. It's like breaking a leg, it doesn't matter what caused it. You've got to get it fixed, have your physiotherapy and think of what you're going to do next. That tends to be the modern approach. Let's improve your life.'

Dr Nias reckons today's Freudians are pursuing an approach that even its propounder began to lose confidence in before his death. 'Even Freud, towards the end of his life, was saying the treatment didn't seem to work,' says Dr Nias. 'Then he argued that that didn't mean the theory had to be wrong, just that the appli-cation of the theory wasn't working for some reason.' There is some doubt, however, over exactly how Freudian Orbach's approach is. American academic Jeffrey Masson, a former director of the Sigmund Freud Archives, turned against psychoanalysis in 1982 and went on to publish *Against Therapy*, a critique of one of the late-twentieth century's biggest growth industries.

Masson met Orbach when they both participated in a broadcast debate and has since offered some assistance to her partner, Joe Schwartz, in his research for a book on the history of psycho-analysis. 'She seemed like a very nice woman,' he says. 'A lot of therapists are nice people, but that doesn't mean that what they do is good for people.' He doubts whether Orbach ever trained as a Freudian analyst, however, and suggests that it was her expertise in the area of eating disorders that attracted Diana.

'Susie Orbach wrote the book, *Fat is a Feminist Issue*, which is very sound,' he says. 'I really believe that women who are overweight at will are obviously dealing with some trauma. It's not just a lack of willpower, or something of that kind, so it's understandable that somebody like Diana would go to Susie Orbach to seek help for that.

'You know the British position. I mean, the only place in the world where my book, *Against Therapy*, is popular is England, but part of the reason for that is that the English are really opposed to any kind of psychological thinking, and that is not my position. The English use phrases like, "Pull your socks up," "Stop complaining" and "Don't seek into the past," with which I totally disagree. It's just that I don't think that the way to do this is via therapy, so I'm totally sympathetic to someone like Diana seeking help, I'm just not sympathetic to the people who offer her help.'

Having said that, Masson reckons her visits to Orbach may well do her some good. 'I would suspect that what Susie Orbach is telling her is that she should try and remember things that happened to her when she was young,' he says. 'I suspect that's what she's doing, and if she is doing that and is not pushing her in any specific direction, but just saying, "Look, I'm willing to listen to you, think about it," that would be a totally good thing to do. I mean that can't do any harm.

'What's dangerous is when you get therapists who have their own agenda. So, if you're visiting a behaviourist, they'll push you in that direction. If you're seeing a psychoanalyst, they want to push you in that direction. Almost every therapist has some particular direction they want to take you in, and it's very rare that someone will just sit back and say, "I really don't know what's happened to you, but something did and I'm willing to listen." That can't hurt anybody.'

Masson disputes Dr Nias's point that therapy all too often involves vulnerable people being asked to dwell in the most traumatic episodes in their lives to date. 'I don't see anything wrong with that,' he says. 'There's nothing wrong with dwelling as long as you don't have someone pushing you on how to dwell, where to dwell, how long to dwell and what to dwell about. There's no doubt that someone like Diana, Princess of Wales, has some trauma in her past, almost all of us do. So there's clearly nothing wrong with her trying to figure out what it was. What's wrong is when somebody comes along and says, "I know what it was, and I'm going to take you there." Or when anybody pretends to be the expert. If a psychoanalyst is saying, "Look I don't really know what happened to you. Come to me, I'll charge you a reasonable amount of money and try and listen to you and give you some quiet space in which you can think about it," it can't do any harm.'

No one will know more about Diana's innermost thoughts than her psychotherapist. As Orbach's friend Dr Dorothy Rowe says: 'Susie Orbach will never have a quiet life. Susie knows a lot of her secrets, so even if Diana stops seeing her today, Susie is in possession of extremely personal information.'

BOOK TWO

BOOK TWO

SEVEN

THE FORMATIVE YEARS

'A mother cannot help dying, but she can help bolting off with another man.'

Dr Dennis Friedman, psychiatrist and medical director of the Charter Clinic

Diana's childhood is a psychoanalyst's playground. Her mother left the family home after the break-up of her marriage when Diana was six; Diana's father was a detached and bad-tempered parent; she was sent away to boarding school at the age of nine; and she hated the woman her father went on to marry. Ever since Sigmund Freud formulated his psychoanalytic approach at the turn of the century, therapists of all persuasions have recognized that the child is father of the man. The Moravian-born psychiatrist, who practised in Vienna, relied heavily on the analysis of early experiences of trauma, especially sexual trauma, to cure psychological problems in later life.

Given these preoccupations, Freud would have a field day with Diana if he were alive today. Despite being born into material privilege, her emotional suffering began early. After her mother left the marital home, a messy divorce followed. And, far from being a sweet and unassuming child, it is now clear that Diana grew up as an attention seeker and someone who, according to her brother, Charles, 'had real difficulty in telling the truth'. Even her eating disorders date back to her schooldays at West Heath, where she would eat four bowls of All Bran for breakfast and then throw up. This dysfunctional childhood was worsened in adolescence by her father's second marriage to Raine, Countess of Dartmouth, a woman to whom Diana took an instant dislike.

Her childhood discontent has its roots in her parents' unhappy marriage. By the time of Diana's birth in 1961 relations between Johnnie Spencer, who became the 8th Earl Spencer on the death of his father in 1975, and his wife the former Hon. Frances Burke Roche, had already deteriorated badly. Pressure to provide a male heir was intense, until, after producing three daughters, Frances gave birth to Charles, three years after Diana. From there on the marriage began soon to fall apart. Much of the blame for the break-up has been attached to Diana's mother, not least because it was she who left, but it is clear that the earl, outwardly an agreeable host and clubbable squire, had a dark side. According to Lady Colin Campbell, he was a 'wife-beater' with 'a vicious temper and a cruel streak', and there were allegations of cruelty in his spouse's divorce petition.

Frances had first met Peter Shand Kydd, an extrovert businessman 11 years her senior, at a dinner party in London. Shand Kydd had inherited his family's wallpaper business and, at the time of the fateful meeting with Frances, was married to the artist Janet Monro Kerr, with whom he had had three children. Their flirtation turned into a fully fledged affair. While Diana, her sisters and brother remained at Park House, the family home on the Sandringham Estate, her mother was travelling to an address in west London for clandestine meetings with her new lover. A trial separation followed. Sarah and Jane were both away at boarding school by this time, but Diana and her brother, Charles, moved to London with their mother. After returning to spend Christmas at Park House, however, their father refused to allow their mother to leave with them. It was Lord Spencer, then Viscount Althorp, who emerged victorious from the ensuing custody battle conducted behind closed doors in the Family Division of the High Court.

A scandalous divorce action followed in the spring of 1969 when Frances's mother, Ruth, Lady Fermoy, sided with her son-in-law, and, again, Frances suffered a devastating defeat. One of the most remarkable features of the case was that, according to one source, Lord Spencer insisted that his young daughter sit in court to listen to the exchanges between her parents' lawyers. The traumatic effect on Diana of hearing her mother's reputation being demolished in front of her may only be guessed at.

'Frances's divorce action should have succeeded because she had a valid sense of injustice,' says Lady Colin Campbell. 'He had abused her physically and emotionally, and she should have been allowed to divorce him but, of course, the Establishment closed ranks against her, because he was the one who had the title and who stood to inherit the big house. Her own mother joined forces against her because she was such an insuperable snob, being a middle-class girl from an Indian background. Having seen her daughter marry up in the world, she was damned if she was going to sit and watch as she threw up what she regarded as a great prize for a wallpaper merchant.'

The feuding between Diana's parents did not end with the courtroom battles, however. Despite the fact that Lord Spencer had won custody, the children continued to spend much of their time out of school with their mother, and war was continued by other means.

'She would tell them how happy she was to see them, which was fine, but when they left she would cry and carry on,' says Lady Colin, 'telling them how their father was ruining her life. As a result when they went back to their father, Diana and the other children would sulk for the first day or two, and he would indulge them to counteract the effect of the mother's behaviour.

'In fact, both parents made the classic mistake of overindulging the children so there was no real boundaries. Diana was a spoilt brat. On one celebrated occasion her sister Sarah even brought her horse into the drawing room for tea in front of her father and grandmother. That tells you, doesn't it?'

Quite how damaging this upbringing was to prove did not become clear until much later. Dr Dennis Friedman underlines a distinction that may seed itself in the child's mind, regardless of whether it fairly reflects the actual circumstances and motives of the departing mother: 'A mother cannot help dying, but she can help bolting off with another man. When you're a small child it comes to the same thing, but when you grow up you can look at it differently.'

At her tender age Diana was likely to blame herself in some way for the break-up, according to psychologist Susan Quilliam. 'Any separation is going to have an effect,' she says. 'The major effect is that the child thinks it's its fault: What have I done that mummy and daddy are splitting up? What am I doing that is so awful that mummy is walking out and leaving me? If you abandon a child at six months, it will die – so we have it built in both psychologically and emotionally that a young child will kick up a fuss if it's abandoned.

'A young child that doesn't get fed for four hours will scream. A child of six probably couldn't cope on its own and would feel abandoned if its main carer left. Then it would experience panic and anger – strong feelings – because it would be receiving a message of: I must be to blame, I'm at fault. It's almost easier when the child is older; if the child is, say, 14, then it has a basis of sense and meaning to explain what is happening. But, at six, although the child has language, she wouldn't have had the sense and meaning actually to understand why mummy was leaving, and that it's got nothing to do with her.

'So that's the first important piece. The second important piece is going to be that mummy has left, and life will change. There will be an impact on daddy; daddy is obviously going to be affected emotionally. I understand, in Diana's case, that daddy was not massively emotionally demonstrative. So Diana didn't get any messages from daddy – though she might have been getting some emotional communication from her mother who isn't there any more. So the quality of her life will change.'

By this time the first signs of her bizarre relationship with food has become apparent. On one occasion she sent a note home from her preparatory school and first boarding school, Riddlesworth Hall at Diss in Norfolk, demanding: 'Big choc. cake, ginger biscuits, Twiglets.' It made such an impression on her father that he kept the note to his dying day. When she moved in 1974 to West Heath school in Sevenoaks, Kent, her unhealthy appetites became even more obvious. A school friend says they were often able to get her to eat three kippers with six slices of bread for breakfast, earning her a reputation as a glutton and resulting in frequent visits to the matron with stomach ache. It is also clear that she was in the early stages of bulimia. 'We used to throw up together,' says a titled lady who knew Diana well in her teens.

In addition to the psychological battering she took from her parents' split, other aspects of Diana's young life were calculated to exacerbate her condition. Nannies – one of whom would hit her over the head with a wooden spoon if she was naughty – came and went with alarming frequency. In revenge, the children would put pins on their chairs, throw their clothes out of windows and lock them in the bathroom.

Nor did school provide a refuge from her unhappy home life. At Silfield School in King's Lynn, at which Diana and Charles were enrolled by their father in 1968, around the time of his separation from Frances, she and her brother were notorious for being the children of divorced parents at a time when divorce was comparatively rare. Apart from that the school was not an intimidating place, but Diana failed to thrive academically, and her brother dubbed her 'Brian' after the dim-witted snail in the popular children's TV series *The Magic Roundabout*.

By this time Diana was already developing what might be politely termed a talent for exaggeration, a trait that was to endure into adulthood. 'I don't know whether a psychologist would say it was the trauma of the divorce, but she had real difficulty telling the truth, purely because she liked to embellish,' her brother told Diana's biographer Andrew Morton. 'On the school run one day the vicar's wife stopped the car and said: "Diana Spencer, if you tell one more lie like that I am going to make you walk home."'

She was also gaining a reputation as an attention-seeker. If she felt ignored as the rest of the family busily prepared for an outing, she would contrive a way of making herself the centre of attention. One incident involved her spraining her ankle after tripping on the stairs while the household was getting ready for a picnic.

'Every child who suffers a major trauma will try and get attention, but the interesting thing is how they get the attention,' says Susan Quilliam, who writes about such matters in her book *Child Watching*. 'There's absolutely no doubt that Diana was seeking the attention, but so were her sisters and her brother. Now some children will seek attention by being very good, behaving very well. They'll work hard at school, they'll never raise their voices, they'll be so good that you actually want to pick them up and shake them and say, "Get a life."

'Diana sought attention by what I would call playing victim. The important thing is that there's nothing worse about that than about any of the other things she could have chosen to do, like spraying graffiti on the walls or setting fire to the school – but women in general are not encouraged to get attention by competing or by displaying aggression or anger in those ways, and Diana would probably have known that by the time she was 18 months old. But Diana didn't get her attention in those ways; like many other women she chose to get attention by having problems. Such women get depressed, they have physical problems, they get ill or, if they're moderately healthy and haven't learned about depression yet, they will fall over and bang their knees.

'They will be the ones who get their goodies by saying, "I'm hurt, help me," which of course leads us in a direct line to the incident where she allegedly threw herself down the stairs. Then she thought, Let's throw myself down the stairs and see if Charles helps me. The problem is he doesn't because his programming doesn't allow him to step in and rescue. He's not a rescuer. Had he been a rescuer, they might have made it work.'

Dr Dorothy Rowe argues that there can be a much more subtle reason behind children injuring themselves. 'Children are so often told by their parents that they are to blame for something – "You've been such a naughty boy, that's why I've got this terrible headache" – the child gets an extended notion of what it's personally responsible for, and they feel very guilty, and they blame themselves for all sorts of things that the adults do.

'Now, if a child feels extremely guilty – and guilt is the fear of punishment, and it's often a great relief when you're actually punished – they bring the punishment on themselves to get it over with. So, quite often, children who are seen to injure themselves, to fall over for no apparent reason, what they're doing isn't necessarily attention-seeking, it's often self-punishing, particularly when pain is involved. After all, children who just want attention can get that without having to suffer any pain. All they've got to do is knock over mum's favourite vase, make a mess, start yelling, or have a fight with their sister.

'OK, if you fall down you get more sympathy. That's how hypochondriacs are made. They grow up in families where no one pays attention to them unless they're sick, and so there's a lot of people who feel that the way to get care and attention is to be ill.'

At the age of nine Diana had been sent away to school for the first time to Riddlesworth Hall and felt the wrench keenly. She missed her father and told him: 'If you love me, you won't leave me here.' One of the remarkable features of almost all the 89 pictures of Diana as a girl that appeared in Andrew Morton's semi-authorized biography is that she looks sulky and hostile. Assuming that her strategy in cooperating with Morton was to highlight the role of an unfeeling husband and an unsympathetic royal household in causing her unhappiness, it seems strange that she could not provide a more upbeat portofolio of portraits.

Equally significant is the fact that the late Earl Spencer, who described his youngest daughter as a 'perfect physical specimen' when she was born, had no qualms about handing over a catalogue of pictures – most of them his own work – which proved to the world what an unhappy child and teenager Diana had been. Dr Dennis Friedman finds this telling.

'I would expect her to be sulky and unhappy and angry, because she had a really bad time,' he says. 'There are a lot of them [photographs], and I'm sure she's asking to have her photograph taken, I mean, she obviously didn't run away from the camera. At the same time she may have seen it as a sort of intrusion. Given that her father was the photographer, she must have been looking to him to satisfy her "look at me" need, but he couldn't do it.

'He couldn't give her the admiration that she obviously needed, because he had problems of his own and wasn't available in a way. He was busy running the estate, and I don't think he had much time for Diana. He is said to have had a very difficult personality, he had a temper, he was an aggressive man, so I don't think she got her money's worth out of that relationship. Now she has everybody in the world looking at her, and that's some kind of compensation but not adequate compensation, because it's a bit unpredictable. People can stop looking at her at any particular moment.'

Dr Sidney Crown regards the sheer number of photographs in which she appears unhappy as significant on two counts. 'Not only does it mean she was probably like that as a child, but it suggests there was a problem in the relationship with her father. Part of the received wisdom of relationships is that the relationship with the opposite-sex parent is highly significant with regard to future relationships with the opposite sex, not only because it's the first one but also because it's a very intimate one at a time when the personality is most malleable, the first five years of life. So it means that she might have less trust in the future and more difficulty in establishing relationships, particularly committed relationships. Many people who come to me say, "I'm sociable and friendly. There's no problem at the office, but when I try to commit myself it all goes wrong. And that's why I'm here." Then you immediately go into their relationships with their fathers.'

Diana's mood was not helped in the early seventies when 'Acid' Raine first appeared on the scene, after being introduced to Johnnie Spencer by her then husband, the Earl of Dartmouth, who had known Johnnie since their days at Eton together. Spencer was available following the break-up of his marriage, and his home – by then the ancestral house on the Althorp Estate – badly needed an iron lady. Althorp was dirty and badly managed, with the finances in such chaos that there was never enough money to pay the staff. The idea that the free-spending Princess that we know today was ever exposed to financial insecurity may be a hard one to grasp, but it is nevertheless key to an understanding of certain aspects of her behaviour. She saw her father surrounded by the trappings of high living – a fine house, thousands of acres of land, valuable family portraits – and yet without enough cash to meet the bills.

It gave her a preoccupation with money that she still shows in flashes. Diana has an almost obsessive concern with being exploited, whether it be by the paparazzi, who can sell snatched pictures of her for thousands of pounds to the tabloids, or former intimates, such as James Hewitt, who kiss and tell. 'During the years, you see yourself as a good product that sits on a shelf and sells well, and people make a lot of money out of you,' she told *Panorama*.

Even though Raine was to prove to have the business brain required to turn round their father's financial fortunes, the children were not in the mood to make things easy for the couple. The year before she married Johnnie, Charles, then 12, made his feelings clear in a 'vile' letter to his prospective stepmother. Diana, meanwhile, showed characteristic cunning by refusing to put pen to paper herself, getting a friend to do the dirty work in the form of a poison-pen letter. Speeding up the process, in case the Spencer girls tried to dissuade their father from the match, Raine arranged her own fee-less transfer from one earl to the other. As a result Diana and her siblings were not even aware of the discreet register-office wedding until after it had taken place.

On one celebrated occasion Diana pushed her stepmother down a short flight of stairs at Althorp, side-stepped her as she lay on the floor and then marched off without so much as a backward glance. 'It's extremely difficult for any new mother to be accepted,' says Susan Quilliam. 'From what I've seen of Raine Spencer, she wanted it very clearly understood that she and Earl Spencer were a couple, and Diana wasn't going to get any chance to have a mother/daughter relationship; Raine probably would have worked against that, at least for the first couple of years.

'In order to develop, children have to recognize that mummy and daddy are a couple, but they also have to feel part of a larger family, and in this case that was not the message that was being put across, as I understand it. The message that was being put across was that the main bond was between daddy and stepmother, and the children were, to some extent, now sidelined. So I can't in all honesty see anything positive about this for any of the children, particularly Diana. If you take a one year old, very often they are less affected because they haven't got memories. If you take a 14 year old, they can often survive because they can start to understand. But a six year old falls somewhere in between and is going to get the worst of all worlds.'

Quilliam reckons the relationship between Diana and her stepmother was not helped by her long absences at boarding school. 'If you're not living in a family for 52 weeks a year, it's actually quite easy to slide away from relationships,' she says. 'The kids would only have been at home for whatever it was, 12 or 14 weeks each year. If they'd actually been thrown together in the house, they'd basically have had to put up or shut up, and rub along with each other. But, as they were constantly being shipped off to boarding school or shipped off to the nanny, they could avoid and evade actually coming to terms with life at home.'

Diana's response to her unhappy life at home was to blame the woman whom she demonized as the wicked stepmother. Raine bore the brunt of her anger and frustration then, but in later life Diana turned her anger inwards, to the point of cutting herself to exorcize her hurt. To the outsider, growing up in the ermine belt of middle England might have seemed an ideal grounding for a young woman destined to reach the very pinnacle of society. Despite her material advantages, by the time Lady Diana Spencer met Charles, the emotional damage was done. The legacy of an upbringing at the hands of parents at war with each other was a mental pattern so confused that the scene was set for a battle royal long before she entered the Palace bedchamber as the bride of a prince.

EIGHT

BROKEN DREAMS

'Gosh, golly, help, panic.'

Prince Charles must have appeared an impossibly glamorous figure to the young Lady Diana Spencer. She was a teenage kindergarten teacher, he was heir to the most powerful monarchy in the world. She was a shy, awkward girl who hid her puppy fat under what one friend called maternity dresses; he was one of the most eligible bachelors in the land, whose name had been linked to a string of alluring women from actress Susan George and brewery heiress Sabrina Guinness to millionaire's daughter Anna Wallace. But Diana had one thing that none of these high society girls could match: a blameless past. As far as anyone knew she was, to put it crudely, a virgin.

While Charles had first set eyes on Diana when she was just a child playing in her nursery at her parental home in Park House, it was after a famous encounter in a ploughed field near Nobottle Wood near Althorp in the winter of 1977 that he first remarked upon her charms. He described her as 'a very jolly and amusing and attractive 16 year old – I mean, great fun, bouncy and full of life'. The only words the star-struck adolescent could bring herself to utter were: 'just amazing'.

But it was to her eldest sister Sarah that he was first attracted. She wrote herself out of the history books, however, when, asked to comment on her relationship with the Prince, she said: 'It is totally platonic – I think of him as the big brother I never had. I wouldn't marry anyone I didn't love, whether it was the dustman or the king of England. If he asked me, I'd turn him down.' Charles got the message and never did.

After their sister, Jane, had married Robert Fellowes, the 36-year-old son of Sir William Fellowes and then the Queen's assistant private secretary, Sarah and Diana were invited to join a shooting party at Sandringham in January 1979. Diana proved a hit with her sister's ex, and, when they returned to London, Charles began to ask her out. It was not long before Diana met the woman who was to be her nemesis, Camilla Parker Bowles. It was Mrs Parker Bowles, already Charles's adulterous lover, who fostered their romance in the belief that the malleable Diana would pose no threat to their illicit affair.

Public testimony to Diana's eligibility came when her uncle, Lord Edmund Fermoy, vouched for her chastity, saying: 'Diana, I can assure you, has never had a lover.' Since then, however, it has become clear that Diana had a number of boyfriends before her marriage, including James Gilbey. When asked by the authors whether he had been Diana's lover prior to her marriage, he replied intriguingly: 'I have no idea.' Other names linked to her before she met Charles were the Hon. George Plumptre, third son of farmer and obscure peer Lord FitzWalter, and Rory Scott, a lieutenant in the Royal Scots Guards. But, in 1980, she was seen as pure as the driven snow. The Palace considered this a jewel beyond price; in demanding a virgin bride, though, they also landed themselves with that most dangerous of things: an unknown quantity.

Charles was obviously aware of the pitfalls. 'You can afford to make a mistake,' he told one journalist at a reception on the lawns of the British High Commission in New Delhi ten months before he married, 'I've got to get it right first time.' Quite how badly he had got it wrong was not to emerge until some time later. For, while Diana may have come across as a brainless young Sloane Ranger, she was soon to emerge as a calculating woman who was to prove more than a match for her husband.

Susan Quilliam reckons that even as she walked down the aisle, Diana was far from being a lamb to the slaughter. 'This was not the blushing bride to the king's altar,' she says. 'He saw her. She went out with him. She felt at ease with him. She felt she could make it work. I have no idea whether if she felt she couldn't make it work she would have had the courage to say no, but I think Charles would have sensed that. She was thoroughly vetted, and the powers-that-be thought it was a suitable match.

'The two of them together might have made it work if they had changed sufficiently to fulfil each other's needs. Diana might have triggered Charles into being more emotionally forthcoming. He's totally withdrawn, he's a withholder. But we also have evidence that he isn't a total "English wet fish". They have a lot in common. He's sensible, he's moderately intelligent. He does have this odd thing about talking to plants, so the man is not totally without sensitivity. He's not a brute. And, therefore, had there been the right things in Diana to bring Charles out, and had there been the right things in Charles to help Diana mature, they could have made a good working marriage of it. I've seen people make it work with a much worse start in life.

'They may have chosen each other for the wrong reasons, but it wasn't necessarily doomed from the start. I'm not blaming the Palace mafia but had they had the normal sort of relationship where she could go to the kitchen and say to her mother-in-law, "Hell, what do you do with him when," and she could have replied, "Oh, don't worry, just let him sulk," things might have been different. But she couldn't go to anybody and say, "I'm married to the Prince of Wales, and he won't give me attention."'

Quilliam, nevertheless, feels Diana accepted the hand of a future king for all the right reasons. 'She went into that marriage wanting to succeed,' she says. 'Not only for herself – because it would make her feel good – she wanted to do right by the country. She wanted to feel good about herself by doing right by her husband and by her country. With Diana it's "Won't it be great, I'll be able to serve as a princess." So there is a streak of selflessness there.

'She went into the marriage quite happy that she was going to be groomed and paid a lot of attention, and she put a lot of effort into finding out how to get it right. But what she learned very, very quickly – and this will almost certainly have added to the eating disorder – was she also had to look glamorous. She had to look good on front covers, and, the way I see it, that added to the bulimia. Having just stuffed herself with 14 bowls of muesli or whatever she would have stopped and thought, What am I doing? That would be the extra kick: Not only will he not love me if I'm fat, but they, the public, won't love me if I'm fat.'

This was certainly a preoccupation of Diana at this time. As she told *Panorama*: 'I was a fat, chubby 20 year old, and I couldn't understand the level of interest.'

From the outset it had been clear that Prince Charles did not share the ardour of his young bride-to-be. While she responded with an enthusiastic, 'Yes,' when photographers at an engagement day photocall asked if they were in love, her fiancé looked distinctly uncomfortable and said wearily, 'Yes, whatever *that* is.' With hindsight this can perhaps be seen as a concession to the feelings of Camilla Parker Bowles, the woman he really loved, whom he knew would be watching the scene on television. According to historian Ben Pimlott's biography, *The Queen*, Charles's mother encouraged his marriage to the 'adolescent' Diana Spencer in the hope of ending his potentially scandalous affair with the wife of a man who had close connections to the Royal Family.

But Diana had no doubts. Some 14 years later, when she got her chance to talk publicly for the first time about the pressures that went with marrying into the Royal Family, she said: 'At the age of 19, you always think you are prepared for everything, and you think you have the knowledge of what's coming ahead. But although I was daunted at the prospect at the time, I felt I had the support of my husband to be.'

She was determined not to duplicate her own unhappy family background. 'I think, like [in] any marriage, specially when you've had divorced parents like myself, you'd want to try even harder to make it work,' she said. 'And you don't want to fall back into a pattern that you've seen happen in your own family. I desperately wanted it to work, I desperately loved my husband, and I wanted to share everything together, and I thought we were a very good team.' The odds were against them from the start, however. Divorce statistics show that the products of broken homes are more likely to split up than those whose parents stayed together.

'The children of broken marriages, or marriages that are in a constant state of conflict, do seem to have more difficulty in making and establishing committed relationships, and there is more likelihood of them separating,' says Dr Sidney Crown, 'whether it's by divorce, or just by dropping out. Diana illustrates that very well because she's got a very disturbed background.'

In Diana's case there was an additional burden: the onerous demands of what she herself calls the 'top job'. 'I wasn't daunted,' she told Martin Bashir, during the *Panorama* interview, 'and am not daunted by the responsibilities that that role creates. It was a challenge, it is a challenge. As for becoming Queen, it was never at the forefront of my mind when I married my husband: it was a long way off, that thought. The most daunting aspect was the media attention, because my husband and I were told when we got engaged that the media would go quietly, and it didn't. And then when we were married they said it would go quietly, and it didn't. And then it started to focus very much on me, and I seemed to be on the front page of a newspaper every single day, which is an isolating experience, and the higher the media put you, place you, is the bigger the drop. And I was very aware of that.'

Diana has a point. For until she arrived on the scene, the media's coverage of the royal had only just shifted from the forelock-tugging to the mildly independent. Edward VIII's affair with Mrs Wallis Simpson in the thirties may have been common knowledge in the United States, but his subjects were the last to learn about it thanks to a cosy relationship between the newspaper owners and the royal household.

The first signs of anyone breaking ranks came in the sixties when writer and broadcaster Malcolm Muggeridge wrote an article in the *Saturday Evening Post* entitled DOES ENGLAND REALLY NEED A QUEEN? Lord Altrincham followed this up with an attack on her 'tweedy, elitist court' in the *National English Review*. Far from opening the floodgates, however, these brave forays led to both men being ostracized, and Altrincham, who had gone so far as to call the Queen 'a priggish schoolgirl, captain of the hockey team, a prefect and a recent candidate for Confirmation', had his face slapped in the street by an outraged royalist.

But by the time Diana began courting Charles, however, the rules of the game had been relaxed. Buckingham Palace's view of the press was undergoing radical change. For years it had viewed newspapers as coarse and intrusive irritants but was now beginning to see them as a potentially valuable tool in the battle against growing public indifference to the monarchy and increasing resentment at the funding of such a costly anachronism.

The younger generation had found its own heroes. While the Queen could once expect to be mobbed by cheering crowds, her popularity was now being eclipsed by rock stars, film actors and television personalities. So the royals decided to get media-friendly. But alongside the meet-the-people walkabouts grew a journalistic tradition that was far different from the deferential approach of old. So, when news broke of Diana's involvement with the most famous bachelor in the world, a phalanx of photographers camped on the doorstep of her London apartment block, and teams of reporters stalked her as she hovered on a river bank dutifully pretending to take an interest in her royal boyfriend's fly fishing.

It was this policy of engagement with the media that proved Diana's undoing, according to psychiatrist Dr Dennis Friedman, rather than any outstanding feature of her personality. 'She's only remarkable because the *Sunday Mirror* and the *Sun* weren't available in 1840,' he says.

'She's not behaved any differently from any of the others. Edward VII had dozens of relationships outside his marriage. The Duke of Clarence used homosexual brothels. I suppose George V and Queen Mary got on reasonably well with each other, but that was a very formal, stuffy sort of marriage. George V was terribly aggressive to his children. They were more or less brutalized by him. Edward VIII had lots of girlfriends before he ended up with Mrs Simpson. There have been lots like that, I don't think Diana is particularly spectacular in that respect. Queen Alexandra was the Diana of her day. She was a fashion plate. She was admired, everybody loved her. She was treated badly by Edward VII. I think there's nothing new, frankly, but it's just what we read about it.'

The obsessive interest shown in Diana and Charles's very twentieth-century courtship failed to take the edge off a heady romance, but it was not long before it had an entirely unexpected effect, as Diana revealed on *Panorama*.

MARTIN BASHIR: 'At this early stage, would you say that you were happily married?'

DIANA: 'Very much so. But the pressure on us both as a couple with the media was phenomenal and misunderstood by a great many people. We'd be going round Australia [Alice Springs, where, in particular, Diana first realized clearly how popular she was with the public] for instance, and all you could hear was, "Oh, she's on the other side." Now, if you're a man, like my husband a proud man, you mind about that if you hear it every day for four weeks, and you feel low about it, instead of feeling happy and sharing it.'

BASHIR: 'When you say, "She's on the other side," what do you mean?'

DIANA: 'Well, they weren't on the right side to wave at me or touch me.'

BASHIR: 'So they were expressing a preference even then for you rather than your husband?'

DIANA: 'Yes – which I felt very uncomfortable with, and I felt it was unfair, because I wanted to share.'

BASHIR: 'But you were flattered by the media attention particularly?'

DIANA: 'No, not particularly, because with the media attention came a lot of jealousy, a great deal of complicated situations arose because of that.'

This all strikes a chord with Dr Crown. 'Somehow Charles's personality didn't appeal to people very much, he was always trying to find a way in which he could appeal to them, but it didn't work,' he says. 'They laughed at him, and I think that he would be very jealous, very envious of her success in that context. When he comes along, people groan. And when she comes along they all cheer. I think it's his negative attitude and inability probably to share in his partner's success. If someone does well you congratulate them and feel pleased about it. I doubt whether he was ever pleased about anything she ever did. He was rather resentful and envious of her, so in that sense, yes, that unrewarding part of the relationship has compounded her problems.'

Diana claimed to have been bemused by her instant popularity. 'Well, it took a long time to understand why people were so interested in me,' she said, 'but I assumed it was because my husband had done a lot of wonderful work leading up to our marriage and our relationship.'

Things were not made any easier for Diana by the fact that she was given so little guidance in how to conduct herself. She certainly feels this was the case. 'Yes, I do, on reflection,' she told *Panorama*. 'But then here was a situation that hadn't ever happened before in history, in the sense that the media were everywhere, and here was a fairy story that everybody wanted to work. And so it was, it was isolating, but it was also a situation where you couldn't indulge in feeling sorry for yourself: you had to either sink or swim. And you had to learn that very fast.'

This refusal to offer any sort of training to its most high-profile recruit is entirely typical of the Royal Family's myopic approach to the modern world, according to Dr Sidney Crown. 'I think the whole business with the Royal Family is that they never seem to do any sensible thinking about broad psychological issues,' he says. 'I think they are psychologically illiterate, and it wouldn't matter if they were protected, like Henry VIII was, but Diana has entered the family at a time when everything has become democratized in a sense, and yet they still go on as if these things can be picked up along the way. If you're born into the Royal Family, you are groomed, but she came into it late with no training and had to find her own strategy, and yet she blossomed.

'The incident at Alice Springs illustrates it very well. People actually do take to her. They like her smile. They like her looks. I only saw her close up once, and that was long before her problems became public. She was then extraordinarily attractive in public, you could really warm to her, and she did it [all] very well. Her success reinforced her confidence, so she repeats the same sort of behaviour over and over again. If a certain type of behaviour is rewarded you repeat it, and the unsuccessful ones you wipe out. Prince Charles never found an initial strategy like that, and he became less and less popular. That's one of his problems.'

Auberon Waugh, the editor of the *Literary Review*, is one who counts himself as a fan. As an acerbic columnist he deflates politicians on a daily basis and is a scourge of the politically correct, but by Diana he has been totally disarmed. 'When you meet her you realize she isn't as described: this evil, manipulative cow,' he says.

'She's a sincere, very charming and rather admirable person. I honestly think it's as straightforward as that.'

'She came and gave away the prizes for the *Literary Review* poetry prize. I'd met her once before, and one is a bit prepared to be impressed when you meet almost any member of the Royal Family, but I found her amazingly frank and upfront in saying what she thought.'

The strains caused by Diana's growing popularity soon spilled over into the marriage. 'Well, we were a newly married couple so obviously we had those pressures too,' she said. 'And we had the media, who were completely fascinated by everything we did. And it was difficult to share that load, because I was the one who was always pitched out front, whether it was my clothes, what I said, what my hair was doing, everything – which was a pretty dull subject, actually, and it's been exhausted over the years – when actually what we wanted to be, what we wanted supported was our work, and as a team.

'It [the press interest] made it very difficult, because for a situation where it was a couple working in the same job – we got out the same car, we shook the [same] hands, my husband did the speeches, I did the handshaking – so basically we were a married couple doing the same job, which is very difficult for anyone, and more so if you've got all the attention on you. We struggled a bit with it, it was very difficult; and then my husband decided that we do separate engagements, which was a bit sad for me, because I quite liked the company. But there again I didn't have the choice.'

By this stage it was obvious to both of them that they had little in common. Indeed, Charles was to say as much himself to his biographer Jonathan Dimbleby in 1994. But Diana insisted on *Panorama* that they shared many interests. 'We both liked people, both liked country life, both loved children, work in the cancer field, work in hospices,' she said.

Nevertheless it is said that Diana was less content at their Georgian country residence, Highgrove, in Gloucestershire, and, whenever she visited, couldn't wait to get back to her London home in Kensington Palace, close to her beloved Harvey Nichols and San Lorenzo. 'Standing in a grass butt in the hills for hours, waiting for the pheasants to rise is a wonderful time for two people in their kind of position to be together and relaxed,' a friend of the Prince, speaking with his knowledge, told the authors. 'But she never wanted to be part of that. She made no effort, and I find that very sad. Polo, fishing, hunting and shooting are his interests, and she always knew that. I haven't seen any marriage work in these circles where the wife hasn't shared the husband's activities.'

But while Charles's confidante reveals her lack of interest in his hobbies, according to Diana, he was not the kind of man to share in any of her pursuits. 'I don't think I was allowed to have any,' she told *Panorama*. 'I think I've always been the 18-year-old girl he got engaged to, so I don't think I've been given any credit for growth. And my goodness, I've had to grow.'

Not only would her husband fail to encourage her, but on the occasions when she did achieve something it was met with indifference, and when she went wrong she was made aware of it in no uncertain terms. 'Anything good I ever did nobody ever said a thing, never said, "Well done," or "Was it OK?,"' she said. 'But if I tripped up, which invariably I did, because I was new at the game, a ton of bricks came down on me . . . . Obviously there were lots of tears, and one could dive into the bulimia, into escape.'

The one man who remained immune to Diana's undoubted charms, and the appealing side of her nature that drew the public to her, was her own husband. The couple had not even completed their honeymoon when Diana claims to have discovered that, far from ending his affair with Mrs Parker Bowles, Charles had every intention of continuing it as if nothing had happened. The situation merited Diana's most carefully honed soundbite.

'Well, there were three of us in this marriage so it was a bit crowded,' she told *Panorama*, with a grin of resignation that was almost feline. Before this Diana was reported to have said that, during a bitter quarrel, Charles had told her that his father had said he could go back to his bachelor ways if, after five years, the marriage was not working.

At the root of this, and every marital break-up, says Dr Sidney Crown, is sex. 'When you are dealing with sexual and relationship problems, you usually find they are related, and sexuality is like a barometer or chemical indicator of other aspects of the relationship,' he says. 'People say things like, "He never kisses me in the kitchen when he comes home from work, so I won't make love to him tonight." You sometimes get a pure sexual problem, which is to do with the sexual mechanics, and, when evaluated, the rest of the relationship seems to be as good as it could be.

'After all, sex is a learned thing. I mean, the potential is natural, but the actual technique is learned, and people either learn it or don't learn it for all sorts of reasons. One reason some don't learn it is inhibition, which makes it very difficult for some people to be entirely relaxed, although that's changed over the years because of all the magazines and discussion programmes that make it easier for people to talk about things.

'I think that for a royal and the partner of his choice there must be enormous difficulty in being spontaneous. I would guess that a royal might never bother to learn the technique of pleasing a woman because he was so eligible, if you like. It comes down to arrogance really. Arrogance that goes right through the royals and upper-class people in general. They do feel they are, in a sense, God's gift, who probably aren't very receptive to being criticized. One would feel that he, in particular, might be very sensitive, because his whole life has been spent under a number of clouds and problems, like a domineering mum and a domineering grandmother, and a dad who stomps around the place wanting him to do military things. I would think that he would lack confidence, and that would spill over into the sexual area. And, in a sense, that would fit also into Camilla being an older woman, a more experienced woman, who would be a good sex therapist.

'I think Camilla probably loved him and would have been prepared to take the trouble to teach him. By then it was too late to go back to rekindle the Diana situation. By the time he was more sexually competent, the relationship between him and Diana had deteriorated so much that he would be unlikely to want, or be able, to carry what he'd learned through in the relationship with her. I'm always dealing with people who have extra-marital affairs, and although they have the particular sex thing with their mistress, they also take trouble with their wife, even if the heart's not entirely in it. One wonders whether Charles would do that. I'm suggesting that what he learned with

Camilla he would have been unlikely to pass on to Diana.' But once the sexual side of their marriage had broken down, would Diana have accepted Charles finding an outlet in Camilla?

'We don't know whether she did for a time,' he says. 'Now she's saying it's such a lousy marriage and always has been, implying she never accepted it. I would have guessed at the time that she may not have accepted it, but she would have lived with it, put up with it for the sake of the whole scene, really her being a super royal, if you like, and still with a future in that area.'

More than one of Charles's friends told the authors that, despite her apparent compliance, Diana was only biding her time. But Susan Quilliam traces the behaviour back to her childhood feelings of rejection. 'Initially she was a superbly biddable pupil,' says Quilliam. 'She obeyed. She said: "What do you want of me? Fine I'll do it." That's another way of reacting to a childhood problem, an abandonment such as Diana underwent – "What do you want me to do? OK, I'll be good."

'So she followed the rules, and she followed them and followed them, but however good she was she still wasn't getting what she wanted, which was Charles's love and support and adoration. And the problem is that however supportive he might have been, I have a feeling that she would never have got what she wanted, because Diana wanted everything all the time; she had a big need. So then her whole motivation changes, and it becomes not just a case of being good for Charles, but being good because she feels better about herself, and she looks good, so she gets more attention. She's constantly striving, she's a perfectionist.

'She drives herself to go to the gym, she drives herself on the eating, she pushes and pushes and pushes, and it's all underpinned by distress. And, in all honesty, on the basis of her comments in the *Panorama* interview this is not a woman, for me, who is at ease with her sexuality. I wouldn't say that a woman who dresses sharply and elegantly is therefore not at ease with her sexuality, but with Diana I don't think sex is where her motivation comes from. I think she's got a very clear and very accurate idea of what her public wants from her, and she's fulfilling it. She looks well groomed, she looks elegant, she looks slim, she's everybody's fairytale princess.'

Whatever the turmoil in their relationship, to the outside world that fairytale image remained intact in those early years, and when she became pregnant it seemed further evidence that the royal marriage was on course. What's more she learned she was going to provide the Royal Family with the necessary male heir at the first time of asking. Invited to give her reaction to the news that she was going to have a boy, she replied: 'Enormous relief. I felt the whole country was in labour with me. Enormous relief. But I had actually known that William was going to be a boy, because the scan had shown it so it caused no surprise.'

Her own traumatic childhood had not put her off the idea of having a family of her own. 'I came from a family where there were four of us, so we had enormous fun there,' she said. 'Then William and Harry – arrived fortunately two boys: it would have been a little tricky if it had been two girls – but that in itself brings the responsibilities of bringing them up, William's future being as it is, and Harry like a form of back-up in that aspect.'

But while the arrival of the two boys confirmed the public in the view that this was a model royal family, beneath the surface tensions were mounting. Newspaper reports that Diana in private was a very different person from the charming figure she presented in public began appearing in the mid-eighties. French papers suggested she was 'a determined and domineering woman'. In an interview with ITN's Alastair Burnet she was asked whether she was hurt by these allegations: 'Well, obviously, you feel very wounded,' she said. 'You think, oh gosh, oh golly, I don't want to go out and do my engagements this morning. Nobody wants to see me, help, panic.'

By the late summer of 1987 the couple had begun the longest estrangement to date in their troubled marriage. They did not see each other for five weeks while Charles stayed at Balmoral or Birkhall, the Queen Mother's house on Deeside, and Diana remained at Kensington Palace. Speculation about the state of the marriage was heightened when it was learned he had spent part of his Scottish sojourn in the company of his much loved friend 'Kanga', Lady Dale Tryon. Diana shrugged off the controversy with an ill-judged remark. 'When we first got married we were everyone's idea of the world's most ideal, perfect couple,' she said. 'Now they say we're leading separate lives. The next thing I know, I'll read in some newspaper that I've got a black lover.'

As time went on it became obvious to those close to the Royal Family that the couple were leading more and more separate lives. And Diana was not only isolated from her husband but, increasingly, from the rest of his family. A remark about the Queen Mother made during her recorded conversation with James Gilbey, revealed just how socially under siege Diana felt: 'His grandmother is always looking at me with a sort of strange look in her eyes. It's not hatred, it's a sort of interest and pity mixed in one. I'm not quite sure how to understand it. Every time I look up she's looking at me and then looks away and then smiles.'

Princess Margaret later summed up the family's feelings, when she told a small gathering of friends at Bowood House, the Earl of Shelburne's mansion in Wiltshire: 'We are very glad to have got rid of Diana.'

Even at this stage, however, it might still have been possible to maintain the public fiction of togetherness. But Diana insisted that this was not an option. 'No, because again the media was very interested about our set-up, inverted commas,' she said. 'When we went abroad we had separate apartments, albeit we were on the same floor, so, of course, that was leaked, and that caused complications. But Charles and I had our duty to perform and that was paramount.' Any prospects of a reconciliation were damned by the publication of Andrew Morton's *Diana, Her True Story* in June 1992. Thanks to the Princess's full, if indirect, cooperation, it told the inside story of the war between the Waleses, detailing Charles's infidelity with Mrs Parker Bowles.

As Diana told *Panorama*: 'Well, what had been hidden or rather what we thought had been hidden then became out in the open and was spoken about on a daily basis, and the pressure was for us to sort ourselves out in some way. Were we going to stay together or were we going to separate? And the word separation and divorce kept coming up in the media on a daily basis .... We struggled along. We did our engagements together. And, in our private life it was obviously turbulent.'

Within months it was clear that, despite the pressure on him to maintain the marriage at all costs, Charles had had enough. All passion spent, they sat down to organize their separation. 'My husband and I, we discussed it very calmly,' said Diana. 'We could see what the public were requiring. They wanted clarity of a situation that was obviously becoming intolerable.'

In December 1992 the separation was duly announced. Lord Archer remembers the occasion well. 'The announcement was made in the House of Lords by the Lord Chancellor,' he says. 'I'll never forget it because the Lord Chancellor rose from his seat, something he never does. He sits there like a great turnip on the end of his red cushion and never moves. He got up, and the whole House was astonished. Everyone stopped talking and looked at him, and he said: "I have an announcement from Her Majesty the Queen, from Buckingham Palace. My Lords, she wishes you to know," and on he went. I remember being stunned that this was actually the way it was done: the Queen informs the Lord Chancellor, the Lord Chancellor informs the Lords and then the Prime Minister, so I rushed around to the Prime Minister's office. I knew I was going to be with Diana at a luncheon the following day.'

On the day the separation was announced in the Lords, Diana was on an engagement 'up North'. And, always the mother hen, she was later keen to make it clear that even at this difficult time she had the welfare of her children very much at heart. Both were boarders at Ludgrove prep school when the news broke.

'Yes, I went down a week beforehand and explained to them what was happening,' she said. 'And they took it as children do. Lots of questions and I hoped I was able to reassure them. But, who knows?' Concern for 'my boys' is one of the themes that runs through Diana's justification of her role in the royal marriage break-up. She is at pains to point out that she made great efforts to keep them informed and comfort them at each stage. But it is clear that she had an almost unhealthy reliance on them for emotional support. 'You do love me more than daddy, don't you,' she is once alleged to have asked her sons as she put them to bed.

Dr Crown comments: 'The nicest part here is that she loves them and wants to do the best by them, but then you get on to more murky parts. The first thing is that it has always been a terribly competitive thing with Charles and, either because their respective advisors or their natural instincts, they have always tried to show themselves doing different things with the children. Whether it's just taking them to school or doing the things that Charles does, which always strike me as a mistake, because children don't like hunting, shooting and fishing.

'You do find that in broken marriages people do put on to the children the most awful dilemmas – like one parent saying, "You do love me more than your father don't you?" What is the child to say? There is no answer. When they are so young and naïve it would put a terrible strain on them. It produces what is technically called a "double bind". What that actually means is that you're put in a position of conflict, where both the alternatives are terribly important to you, and you can't resolve them. It's terribly stressful for the children, some are resilient, and some are not. On the whole children are more resilient than you think they will be, but it doesn't mean they won't be scarred. When they are 18 or 20, they will say to their first girlfriend, "Mummy used to ask if I liked her more than daddy. It was bloody awful." I think it would be most likely that they will have quite a few problems when they're a bit older.'

William, at the age of 10, was already shouldering an enormous emotional burden. He loved his father dearly yet could not understand Charles's indifference towards his mother, whom he could see was deeply upset. Neither he nor Harry could have failed to sense the atmosphere of bitterness that prevailed whenever their parents were together. In the weeks, months and years that followed, they saw the battle played out publicly on television and in the newspapers and were made brutally aware of Charles and Diana's affairs with other people.

So how much damage has been done to the young Princes? 'I've got two answers to that,' says Susan Quilliam. 'The first one is I don't see there's much of a problem. I look at them. I look and I look and I look, because I'm thinking they can't be coming out of all this unscathed. No one can come out of this unscathed. But, in all honesty, I can't see a single example of the young Princes in public being anything other than a nice, well brought-up, well-behaved couple of boys, yet I don't believe it.

'There's got to be something. So I'm very confused. The thing is that not everybody who goes through a childhood trauma becomes distressed by it. Some people who have been through very minor traumas are extremely depressed, and some people who go through very major traumas learn to ride them emotionally. So we are not talking an inevitability of two screwed-up little boys.

'If we were having this conversation some way down the road about the break-up of Harry's marriage, we could say quite definitely that we could trace it back to Diana and Charles. I have absolutely no doubt that there is a tremendous struggle between them [for the boys' affections]. But the boys must have suffered from the fact that Charles, though an affectionate father, is not a particularly emotional father. They've almost certainly been affected by having a mother with a huge personality, who is very emotionally demanding. One thing that can happen next, for example, is that, because personality traits can skip a generation, it could be that both boys could have the emotional solidity of the Queen or the Queen Mother, in which case they'll be riding with the blows from Diana. They love her very much, and they are handling the problem because, after all, most of their schoolfriends probably have divorced parents anyway.

'It depends who they marry. One or even both of them might, for example, choose to marry extremely dominant, vibrant, neurotic women, because they want to do it again with mummy and get it right. Charles's relationship with Diana would have been stable for life if she had played by the old rules, but she's a new woman and she'd read the sort of books that I write about "Don't put up with your husband having an affair," and she thought they applied to her. Well, now they do, but they didn't then because she was a princess, and princesses put up and shut up.'

But what if she had not been a princess? What if she had married a stockbroker and lived in the Home Counties? Would her life have been very different? 'The difficulties in her upbringing, the difficulties in forming relationships with her mother and father and so on, they would all still be with her,' says Dr Crown. 'She's the sort of person one sees in ordinary practice who can't make relations with her peers, and we'd try to work on that. It wouldn't be dramatized by her being a public figure, which would be the only difference. But I don't think there is any suggestion that she wouldn't have got into the same sort of problems. The roots are there, it just wouldn't all come out in such a theatrical and public form.

'Many of the people that I see from that sort of background –

the husband works in the City, they've got a nice house in Haywards Heath, they've got a BMW – they survive, and they're OK. If they're bad-tempered with the au pair it doesn't make headlines. I believe that Diana would have survived that much more easily, but I still don't think that she would ever have been the easiest person to live with.'

Dr Friedman agrees that without the incessant scrutiny that comes with their lofty position, things might have been easier for plain Charles and Diana Windsor. 'I think the media have stirred the whole thing up. Without the glare of publicity, without the goldfish-bowl effect, without the 600mm Nikon lenses, I think she and Charles would have had a few screaming matches and might well have come to some sort of *modus vivendi* that would have worked for them. But they can't, it's all in public. If she'd married a stockbroker, she could have been in a reasonably stable relationship.'

Even marrying into the Royal Family at a lower level would have given her a better chance of survival, according to Dr Crown. 'She is very senior in royal life, and if you go down to the periphery characters in the Royal Family, many of them are perfectly happy in ordinary jobs of various sorts,' he says. 'But she gets this, what I always think of as, an arranged marriage with Charles, and so she's projected to the very top as a potential queen, and that focused enormous attention on her, not just from the media in her own country but from all over the world. It's impossible to conceive what the effect must be like even if you're a very strong person. So it's the intensity of her position as wife of the heir to the throne, which is quite different from being just another royal.'

But, even so, can the media be held solely responsible for the breakdown of the marriage? Dr Friedman doesn't think so. 'It's very damaging, but I suppose in some ways it's better than nothing, because it's better to be noticed than ignored,' he says. 'On the other hand, if you're noticed by the cameras and the press, you're less inclined to work at being noticed by your husband, and if there wasn't all this media attention she would deal with her needs either in therapy or counselling, or just talking with her partner and trying to work out how they can help each other.'

As she experienced more and more depression and turbulence

in her own life, Diana was well qualified to deliver a speech at a Turning Point conference on women and mental health in 1993. She had never appeared more in tune with a message she was delivering than when she said that women should not have to sacrifice everything for their loved ones and live in the shadow of others 'at the cost of their health, their inner strength and their own self-worth'.

She spoke of 'the haze of loneliness and depression' that drove women to tranquillizers, sleeping pills and antidepressants, and came up with the interesting phrase 'anxious zombies'. As if to drive the point home, she concluded: 'Health and happiness taken at the cost of others' pain and suffering cannot be acceptable. Women have a right to their own piece of mind. Each person is born with very individual qualities and potential.' It was those 'very individual qualities' that she utilized so effectively in her fight back.

REVENGE

'She's damaged for life. She ought to be pitied.'

DAVID MONTGOMERY, CHIEF EXECUTIVE, MIRROR GROUP NEWSPAPERS

Diana's expertise in the use of the media had been honed over 11 years as the most photographed and written about woman in the world. By 1991 she was ready to make full use of the power her enormous popularity gave her in the battle against her unfaithful husband and the Palace machine that backed him. The man she picked to expose the inner workings of what she saw as a marriage made in hell was, improbably enough, a former royal reporter for the *Daily Star*, Andrew Morton, who had since become a freelance journalist and author. Through her brother and a select group of trusted friends, she indirectly supplied Morton her account of life in the Royal Family. Not only did it alert the world to the hopeless state of the royal marriage but it also exposed Charles's ongoing relationship with Camilla Parker Bowles and gave a sympathetic account of her bulimia and her alleged suicide attempts.

Launched on 7 June 1992, within a year it had sold five million copies in twenty languages. In Diana's own words, it left the Royal Family 'shocked and horrified and very disappointed', and the Queen later referred to the year of publication, during which a succession of crises assailed her, as her '*annus horribilis*'. Any lingering doubts over Diana's involvement with the book were dispelled during the television interview that marked the second phase of her counterattack against her husband and his supporters. In an incendiary discussion with Martin Bashir, the following exchange took place:

BASHIR: 'Did you ever meet Morton or personally help him with the book?'

DIANA: 'I never met him, no.'

BASHIR: 'Did you personally assist him?'

DIANA: 'A lot of people saw the distress that my life was in, and they felt it was a supportive thing to help in the way that they did.'

BASHIR: 'Did you allow your close friends to speak to Morton?'

DIANA: 'Yes, I did, yes, I did.'

BASHIR: 'Why?'

DIANA: 'I was at the end of my tether. I was desperate. I think I was so fed up with being seen as someone who was a basket-case because I am a very strong person, and I know that causes complications in the system that I live in.'

The methods Diana chose were, by any standards, devious. When the media storm broke after the first extracts from the book were published in the *Sunday Times*, the Queen's private secretary, Sir Robert Fellowes, confronted Diana and demanded an assurance that she had not cooperated with Morton in any way. Under pressure, she denied any direct involvement, and Fellowes duly passed this on to Lord McGregor, the chairman of the Press Complaints Commission. In a phrase that has entered journalistic folklore, McGregor went on to rebuke the newspapers with his now legendary description of their coverage as 'an odious exhibition of journalists dabbling their fingers in the stuff of other people's souls'.

But evidence of Diana's support came within days when she tipped off photographers that she would be visiting one of the book's key sources, Carolyn Bartholomew. Pictures of her kissing her former flatmate, who had provided information to Morton on some of his most controversial revelations, was a clear endorsement of the book itself. When Fellowes discovered the extent of his sister-in-law's involvement, he was so mortified he offered to resign.

It may have been disloyal; it may have been cunning; it may even have involved economy with the truth; but, as Dr Dorothy Rowe argues, conventional means of retaliation were not open to Diana. 'She was offered the choice of accepting a situation, losing her sense of identity, becoming a nothing, or fighting back,' she says. 'And there's no way you can retaliate and retain your dignity. When you're fighting back you do things that aren't gentlemanly, that aren't what you're supposed to do.'

Forensic psychologist Dr Eric Shepherd picks up on Diana's use of the word 'desperate' to describe the predicament that drove her to conspire with her friends in the production of the Morton book. 'This is the politics of desperation,' he says. 'When you become a chess player, you learn to think several moves ahead. She's not a chess player, but she's trying to be one. The Royal Family, like all major institutions in this country, does a lot of thinking through in terms of game plans. If you've got someone who has a game plan predicated upon desperation and who may not be that intellectual – that is not stupid but not excessively bright – then what you've got is someone who's saying, "What do I do in order to cope with this?" So, a very common human reaction is a knee-jerk response. The person says: "Well, OK, you hurt me, so I'll hurt you."'

Elements of this retaliatory behaviour have leaked out in recent years, including her close associations with certain royal correspondents. But, until now, no major newspaper publisher has ever broken ranks to reveal the full extent of her cooperation with the very media she blames for fomenting her present troubles.

'The thing is that she has manipulated press coverage over the whole period of her troubles,' David Montgomery, chief executive of Mirror Group Newspapers, told the authors, 'that's virtually ten years, I suppose. And in that *Panorama* interview there was no new material. Don't forget that, no new material, just the summary of all her briefings to the press over the years, which had been leaked out through friends or people that she actually knew in the press. All of it was well rehearsed; it was all old . . . . Every scrap of it had appeared. It wasn't fleshed out; it had all been reported in detail everywhere. And a lot of the stuff that had been criticized for being not true and for being scurrilous was absolutely bang on, and the reason it was bang on is because it came from her.'

Stuart Higgins, as editor of the *Sun*, one of the British newspapers that has featured Diana most prominently over the years, agrees that she is an old hand at media manipulation. He cites the occasion when she visited Harefield Hospital to witness a child's heart operation with a camera crew in attendance.

'I think that was a strategic and premeditated attempt to cultivate a certain kind of image, and her decision to allow the TV cameras to do that is a lot different from quietly and discreetly visiting a hospital patient at the dead of night, when there may be publicity some time after,' he says. 'I think she had privately pledged that she would not do any TV appearances, and I believe people are wising up to her. Certainly the reaction from our readers is that they think it was a cynical ploy, so however well meaning she intended it to be, it backfired.'

An early insight into Diana's attitude to the press is illustrated by David Montgomery's recollection of his only encounter with the Princess in 1985, when he was editor of the *News of the World*.

'It was a reception at Buckingham Palace,' he says. 'All the editors were there, [Sir] David English [then the celebrated editor of the *Daily Mail*], the whole swarm of editors. And she and Charles were together, and they had us there to be briefed by the press secretary saying, "They're really nice people. Leave them alone. Everything's wonderful. We'll treat you with respect and let you into all our secrets. Now you can have a nice cup of tea." So we had a nice cup of tea, and Di said, "I've only got one thing to say to you, the *News of the World* is sometimes far too accurate. I'm not happy that our sleeping arrangements are divulged." That was in response to sleeping arrangements of the innocent type. I think it was about how Charles would stay up late listening to opera and would sleep in his study, while she would sleep in the matrimonial bed. We now know, of course, that that was more interesting than we thought it was at the time.

'With all the vision of hindsight I thought that she had seemed to be a rather difficult type of woman, but she would flirt with you and manipulate you if you allowed her to. And, clearly, that became an art form, I suppose. I haven't met her since then. I've had conversations with her through an intermediary, but I've never met her in person. I know she's had Rupert Murdoch in to tea or lunch or whatever. She's had David English in. I think she's had everybody in. But not me. I think actually, I'm the odd one out, and I think that, for whatever reasons, she's avoided me.'

As the stories about her private life became more and more scandalous, the media pressure that she once described as 'relentless' also became unfavourable. She may be reaping what she has sown, but can Diana continue to cope in an increasingly inclement media climate?

'No,' says Montgomery, 'she was an unfortunate woman, ill equipped to have this weight thrust upon her, and she's clearly broken under the strain, hence her behaviour. You'd have to be an extraordinary person to have come through this experience, and she hasn't, not unscathed, you know. She got through it, but she's damaged for life. She ought to be pitied.'

Diana would be the last person to concede that her motives for agreeing to the *Panorama* interview were in any way dishonourable and would balk at the suggestion she was driven to do it by as base an instinct as revenge. When Martin Bashir asked her why she was prepared to be so confessional, she trotted out the familiar refrain that it was designed to help disempowered women everywhere. 'Maybe there's a lot of women out there who suffer on the same level but in a different environment,' she said, 'who are unable to stand up for themselves because their self-esteem is cut into two. I don't know.'

By this time Diana's use of the media had been operating in the same comparatively low-key manner for years. Her road to Damascus in this context occurred on a royal tour down under. 'We went to Alice Springs, to Australia, and we went and did a walkabout, and I said to my husband, "What do we do now?" And he said, "Go over to the other side and speak to them." I said: "I can't, I just can't." He said, "Well, you've got to do it." And he went off and did his bit, and I went off and did my bit. It practically finished me off there and then, and I suddenly realized – I went back to our hotel room and realized the impact that, you know, I had to sort myself out. We had a six-week tour – four weeks in Australia and two weeks in New Zealand – and by the end, when we flew back from New Zealand, I was a different person. I realized the sense of duty, the level of interest, and the demanding role I now found myself in.'

From that day Diana never looked back, and, as her confidence grew, her use of the media became more and more overt. A good example of this came the day she accompanied the Queen and Prince Philip to the Palace of Westminster for the State Opening of Parliament in November 1984. Possibly mindful of her minor role in the day's proceedings, she took the decision to wear her hair up for the occasion with devastating results. The Queen's role in what is, constitutionally, the most important day in her year was virtually ignored as the cameras focused on Diana's new hairstyle. The following day almost every newspaper featured it on the front page. Angered by Diana's perhaps unwitting upstaging of his wife's big day, Prince Philip reportedly told his daughter-in-law: 'This isn't done. You don't put on a new hairstyle when we go to these important do's. It's the Queen's day not yours.'

As time went on, even her sons became involved. As well as being innocent victims in an emotional power play with Charles, William and Harry were also part of a sophisticated beauty contest played out in front of the world's press. While Charles engaged them in highly formal, tweedy leisure activities, Diana encouraged them to dress trendily and took them to theme parks such as Alton Towers.

'She sees that the ordinary folk who are the people she woos so much with this Queen of Hearts business are watching her on television all over the country,' says psychiatrist Dr Sidney Crown. 'It makes sense to them that she takes her sons to things they like doing: the water, the splashing, the slides and roundabouts, while all he does is his horrible upper-class thing that involves cruelty to animals.

'She's made a tremendous thing of that and, I think, success-fully. Pictures of them in jeans and trainers are much more attractive than ones of them dressed up in ridiculous costumes. Everyone thinks of Charles as the future king, so what he does with them can't be that flexible, and Diana capitalizes on that. She's got a sort of innate shrewdness, which doesn't come from intelligence or education or anything else, she's just clever at picking things up like that. She's streetwise.'

As her pulling power increased, it became clear that Diana was stealing the thunder not just from Charles but from the entire Royal Family as well. This fuelled a backlash. The Palace courtiers blocked visits abroad, and access to prestigious public events was denied her. She was eventually limited to a never-ending round of charitable engagements. Worn down by the sniping of her husband's advisors, she fought back in the only way she knew: with a carefully staged media event. At a lunch for Headway, the National Head Injuries Association, attended by 600 people paying £100 a head, she announced she was to withdraw from public life.

'The pressure was intolerable then,' she told *Panorama*, 'and my job, my work, was being affected. I wanted to give 110 per cent to my work, and I could only give 50. I was constantly tired, exhausted because the pressure was just – it was so cruel. So I thought the only way to do it was to stand up and make a speech and extract myself before I started disappointing and not carrying out my work. It was my decision to make that speech, because I owed it to the public to say that, you know, "Thank you, I'm disappearing for a bit, but I'll come back."'

What she actually said was: 'When I started my public life 12 years ago, I understood that the media might be interested in what I did. I realized then that their attention would inevitably focus on both our private and public lives. But I was not aware of how overwhelming that attention would become; nor the extent to which it would affect both my public duties and my personal life, in a manner that has been hard to bear.'

Few were taken in by her blaming of the press for this Greta Garbo act. It is inconceivable that a woman with such a need for media attention would be driven into exile on account of it alone. Whatever the full motivation, the result of her self-imposed purdah was that she became a martyr and wrong-footed her persecutors in the Palace hierarchy.

As she said on *Panorama*: 'You know, the campaign at that point was being successful, but it did surprise the people who were causing the grief. It did surprise them when I took myself out of the game. They hadn't expected that. And I'm a great believer that you should always confuse the enemy.' Asked who the enemy was, she replied: 'Well, the enemy was my husband's department because I always got more publicity. My work was more . . . was discussed much more than him. And, you know, from that point of view, I understand it. But I was doing good things, and I wanted to do good things. I was never going to hurt anyone, I was never going to let anyone down.'

In 1994 she carried out just 10 official engagements, compared with 198 the previous year, and good causes are estimated to have lost revenue of up to £5 million as charity premières were reorganized and ticket prices for fundraising lunches were slashed as the royal crowd-puller was replaced with a less charismatic celebrity. Within a year, however, she was back.

According to Lord Archer, apart from anything else, Diana needed something to occupy her time. 'She's got to do something in life,' he says. 'She can't be a shop assistant at Tiffany's, and she can't become a secretary to someone, and she can't become the head of an organization. None of those is available to her. She can only do that which she's rather good at – in fact, she's a damn sight better at it than anyone else – and that is to turn up at functions and make people pay vast sums of money that they would not have otherwise paid to worthwhile causes.'

Wrong-footing 'the enemy' over her public appearances was not enough to end her harassment at the hands of the Palace hierarchy, however. Diana saw dark forces at work behind the publication of her telephone conversation with James Gilbey. Squidgygate was an acutely embarrassing episode for all concerned. It revealed they talked about masturbation, discussed television personality Sir Jimmy Savile's sexuality and commented on the Queen Mother's disdain for Diana. On *Panorama* she hinted at a conspiracy, saying, 'It was done to harm me in a serious manner.' She also described the stories of 300 nuisance calls to Oliver Hoare as 'a huge move to discredit me'.

But the most vivid expression of her anxiety over the machinations of the intelligence services came in a private conversation with one of her therapists. At the time she was cooperating with Andrew Morton's book on her, Diana lived in fear of being silenced by MI5 or another branch of the security services. It has been made known to the authors that on one shocking occasion, she told the therapist: 'One day I'm going to go up in a helicopter, and it'll just blow up. MI5 will do away with me.'

On the face of it she had good reason to see the hand of 'the enemy' in a number of the incidents that damaged her most. The Squidgygate conversation was recorded by at least two people using radio scanners: retired bank manager Cyril Reenan and 25-year-old typist Jane Norgrove. The conspiracy theory grew out of Reenan's insistence that he had taped the call on 4 January, when it was, in fact, made on New Year's Eve. Journalists noted that he lived just 35 miles from GCHQ and speculated that MI5 or Special Branch had rebroadcast a tape of the conversation as part of a dirty-tricks campaign against the Princess. This theory was undermined when Cellnet, the company that operated the mobile-phone network used by Gilbey to speak to Diana at Sandringham, concluded such an act would have been technically impossible.

Speculation then centred on Diana's phone and the possibility that it might be the subject of an authorized government phone tap. This was denied by Downing Street, and in the absence of any proof from Reenan that he had taped the conversation four days after it took place, or any authoritative leaks from the security services, the story degenerated into a complex technical debate that failed to either implicate or clear the intelligence services.

The Hoare affair was more straightforward. Newspapers were able to reproduce details of the duration of many of the calls, and the precise time at which they were made, alongside leaked details of a police inquiry into Hoare's complaint that he was being harassed by an anonymous caller. The person responsible for the leak was almost certainly a corrupt police officer or telephone-company employee, and Scotland Yard raided the offices of a number of private-detective agencies in London in their search for evidence. One of these raids turned up paperwork showing details of calls from the Palace to Hoare, and a file naming the firm was passed on to the Crown Prosecution Service.

It is against this background that Diana decided it was time to launch a new offensive. This time she opted for the power of television and decided to put herself in the firing line with the notorious *Panorama* interview examined earlier. During this premeditated exhibition of revenge few escaped her withering soundbites. Camilla Parker Bowles – though never mentioned by name by Diana – was blamed for triggering her bulimia. The Royal

Family were criticized for their lack of understanding of her plight. Even the Queen's style of monarchy was called into question.

But she saved her most damaging remarks for the finale of her show, when she cast doubt on her husband's fitness to be king, hinting that if the crown skipped a generation it might be better for all concerned. With carefully chosen words Diana chipped away at her husband's birthright, while displaying to the cameras a face that revealed not an ounce of malice. Vengeance, as they say, is a dish best eaten cold.

Not that Diana was prepared to admit that her intentions were anything other than honourable. Aware that viewers would interpret these remarks as those of a woman scorned, Bashir put it to her that she might be taking the opportunity to get her own back on her husband.

Her reply, which closed the interview, was a masterpiece of pious euphemism. 'I don't sit here with resentment,' she said. 'I sit here with sadness because a marriage hasn't worked. I sit here with hope because there's a future ahead. A future for my husband, a future for myself and a future for the monarchy.'

'She does want to get her revenge, there's no doubt about that,' says Dr Crown. It was, he says, a masterful display of 'intuitive skill that many people have for getting under people's skin which bears no relation to educational level. She's good at that. That's why, I think, the Queen is scared of her.' It is, he says, an instinct that 'scares the top people because she has this ability to say, "Well, that will really get at them," and I think that is a conscious policy on her part.'

Dr Dennis Friedman believes Diana's motives are deep-rooted. 'I think she has very powerful retaliatory feelings of anger and feels she has to retaliate because she feels that things have been done to her that are unfair,' he says. 'She feels that injustices have been done to her throughout her childhood, throughout her marriage, and when you believe that, which I think in her case is true, you have to find someone to retaliate against.

'You use Talion Law: what you do to me, I will do to you. It may not necessarily be the one who did it to you, it might be a scapegoat. In the case of the *Panorama* interview, she was obviously quite angry with Charles, but he could say he was a scapegoat to some extent for what her parents had done to her. On the other hand, he was a natural choice for her to retaliate against because he had in fact turned his back on her. But he was just the last in a long line who had done that. He's getting all the flak. You could say that some of the relationships she's had with other men may have been retaliatory. They have been to show Charles, that, "Yes, I am lovable. You were really stupid to have turned away from me."

'I think she does care about those other men at the time, but there are lots of meanings in those relationships. She doesn't just have the relationship because she's suddenly fallen in love, there are lots of other things going for her in them as well. They are part of this "You did it to me, so I'll do it to you" thing towards Charles. She's looking for someone who'll make it up to her for everything she's missed out on previously. I don't know to what extent she's in the relationship for what she can give it. She's so empty inside that giving is not going to be easy for her.'

Dr Friedman also believes that her confession of the affair with James Hewitt was a slap in the face for Charles. 'I think that she is using the relationships that she has with men as a way of getting back at him,' she says. 'She's saying, "You know, these people love me even though you might not. They know a good thing when they see it." So it is a way of getting back at him.'

So why does Diana feel the need to exact revenge? 'I'd say have a look at the possible reasons for hurt,' says Dr Shepherd. 'If you find an inventory of hurt, then you'll find some explanation for her behaviour . . . . What do people sometimes do in these kinds of situations? People who are up against someone who has all the cards? What you'll find is that, very typically, women experience tremendous distress in a relationship particularly a married relationship where the men in our society have enormous power.

'From 30-odd years of experience of dealing with people in treatment what I would say is this. When you're trying to explain a person's behaviour, it's a good idea to go back and say, "What would I do in her position?" Although that's being solipsistic, what you're doing is you're using something that is very commonsensical.

'What I then do is ask, "What would any woman do in this situation?" What we do know is that we are all victims of our past, but we don't have to be slaves to it. When we are in extreme stress we often become slaves to our past. I'm talking about childhood. Charles's problems about handling relationships are a combination of him having extreme power and being impotent. He can't really call the shots, his mother does. But if you look at the way he's reared, he probably entered this marriage psychologically bruised. She probably entered the marriage psychologically bruised. They've certainly both come out psychologically battered by each other.'

But Diana, though battered, is obviously unbowed. The most chilling passage in the entire *Panorama* interview, from a Palace point of view, was where she said: 'She won't go quietly, that's the problem. I'll fight to the end.'

TEN

MIND AND BODY

'Strenuous exercise in increasing amounts is often central to the maintenance of a psychic balance, as is the denial of food.'

SUSIE ORBACH, THE PRINCESS OF WALES'S PSYCHOTHERAPIST

Whatever indifference the rest of the Royal Family showed to Diana's admission of bulimia and self-mutilation, the experts agree that at the root of these distressing acts lies a serious psychiatric condition. Bulimia is classified as a mental illness by the World Health Organization, and acute cases can be compulsorily detained under the 1983 Mental Health Act. While no one is suggesting Diana should have been locked up, Dr Robert Lefever, as founder of the Promis Recovery Centre and author of *How to Combat Anorexia, Bulimia and Compulsive Overeating*, is uncompromising in his judgement that Diana is an addict and will never be free of her addiction unless she opts for a '12-step programme' and all that entails, including regular attendance at meetings with other addicts.

The gravity of Diana's condition is highlighted by her admission that her eating disorder was combined with self-cutting. According to Hubert Lacey, professor of psychiatry at St George's Hospital Medical School in south London and an expert on eating disorders and self-harm, only 15 per cent of bulimics engage in some form of skin-cutting.

Her bulimia began at school but became 'rampant' – to use the

131

Princess's own word – when she discovered her husband had resumed his affair with Camilla Parker Bowles. This fits into the classic pattern of bulimia, whereby sufferers turn to it for consolation at times of great stress. Discussing her illness in detail, Diana told *Panorama*: 'I had bulimia for a number of years. And that's like a secret disease. You inflict it upon yourself because your self-esteem is at a low ebb, and you don't think you're worthy or valuable. You fill your stomach up four or five times a day – some do it more – and it gives you a feeling of comfort. It's like having a pair of arms around you, but it's temporary. Then you're disgusted at the bloatedness of your stomach, and you can bring it all up again. And it's a repetitive pattern which is very destructive to yourself.'

The Princess's account, according to Dr Sidney Crown, glamorizes a condition that he describes as 'really fairly horrible'. As he puts it: 'A bulimic will go to the fridge and tear a virtually raw chicken apart and eat the whole thing and then vomit it. That's not very romantic really.'

Agony aunt Claire Rayner agrees. She reckons the Princess has been highly irresponsible in the way she has presented her condition to the public. 'I feel very strongly about this,' she says. 'I thought it was a dreadful, dreadful thing that she had made bulimia and anorexia seem glamorous. The message she is sending, in effect, is, "Oh, my dears, don't be bulimic, don't be anorexic or, shock horror, you might finish up like me." It's ridiculous, she has glamorized bulimia, and I'm appalled.'

The physical side-effects of the disorder can be horrific. Vomiting brings up not only the food that has been consumed but also stomach acids. These can cause tooth decay, loss of enamel and gum disease; even bloated skin – oedema – and hair loss. A failure to keep down food can also lead to potassium levels in the blood falling to dangerously low levels. This condition – hypokalaemia – can lead to a wide range of complications including muscle weakness, paralysis, occasional neurological disturbances – such as fits – kidney problems and even heart failure.

And it was just the sort of distressed behaviour Dr Crown describes that Diana indulged in regularly over a period of years, as she succumbed to the pressures of royal life. On one occasion, during a visit to open the mammoth Expo exhibition in Vancouver,

Canada, in 1986, she actually fainted with hunger, and Charles, with a characteristic lack of tact, told her that if she was going to faint she should do so in private.

She spoke about her feelings on these public occasions with Martin Bashir: 'If I'd been on what I call an away-day, or I'd been up part of the country all day, I'd come home feeling pretty empty, because my engagements at that time would be to do with people dying, people very sick, people's marriage problems, and I'd come home, and it would be very difficult to know how to comfort myself, having been comforting lots of other people. So it would be a regular pattern to jump into the fridge. It was a symptom of what was going on in my marriage . . . .

'The cause was the situation where my husband and I had to keep everything together because we didn't want to disappoint the public and yet, obviously, there was a lot of anxiety going on within our four walls. It [bingeing and vomiting] was my escape mechanism, and it worked for me at the time.'

Asked if she sought help from other members of the Royal Family, Diana replied: 'No, you have to know that when you have bulimia you're very ashamed of yourself, and you hate yourself and people think you're wasting food so you don't discuss it with people. And the thing about bulimia is your weight always stays the same, whereas with anorexia you visibly shrink. So you can pretend the whole way through. There's no proof.'

Diana felt she was under pressure from other members of the Royal Family to finish her meals. They would say to her: 'I suppose you're going to waste that food later on.' 'And that was pressure in itself,' she says. 'And, of course, I would because it was my release valve.' It was a release valve that she first used as a teenager at West Heath school. Psychologist Susan Quilliam reckons bulimics are often 'graduate anorexics', and it seems likely that Diana, like her eldest sister, Sarah, suffered from the slimmers' disease before resorting to bingeing and vomiting.

'Many bulimic women are anorexics who have basically got a life but have still got their eating problem,' says Quilliam, 'I have never seen any hard evidence, but it's unusual to suddenly snap into bulimia in your twenties. You usually have a distressed relationship with food from the start. Having said that, the vast majority of women nowadays have a distressed relationship with food. I'm not letting Diana off the hook, but there's so much pressure from the media, even for women like me who can walk down the high street without getting mobbed, to watch their weight. So you want to eat, and then you don't want to eat. And then you eat. And you've still got to stay slim. So even if Diana had been totally well balanced, the pressure on her to look good all the time might have triggered problems. But it's much more likely that she had a history of imbalanced attitudes to food from very early on.

'There are a number of theories about anorexia. Firstly, attention-getting. Secondly, and for me at the moment less convincing, that it is a denial of physical maturity – because it normally comes on at 13 or 14, when girls start having periods, and the female shape changes from boyish to curvy. However tall you are, however slim you are, however much of a model you are, your figure is going to get curvy, and you see those curves developing. At the same time you are told that food makes you curvy, so you don't eat the food.

'The third theory is simply about control. At 13 you are sufficiently out of control of your life to be unhappy. A few years earlier you didn't want to be in control of your life because you wanted to be looked after by mum and dad. Then at 13 or 14 you say, "I want my own life," but actually you can't have it. You are at boarding school, you've got a family to fit in with. You know that if you take to the streets you couldn't cope, particularly if you've had a sheltered life. The only thing you can control is yourself, and one of the main ways of controlling yourself is not to eat, and, my God, that has an impact on those around you. So you can control them as well.'

Diana's explanation that her bulimia was sparked anew by Prince Charles's infidelity rings true with Quilliam. 'What triggers bulimia, in particular, is an upsetting event that makes you feel out of control. What more distressing example of being out of control could there be than having your father figure, Charles, take on a wife figure, Camilla – just as your own father took on Raine Spencer. All of a sudden every single emotion in your body rebels, you panic, you get a total body reaction. So you rush over to the fridge, and you do what you know works, which is to put something in your mouth. What happens is that over the next hour and a half – and it's as quick as that – you think, Oh, my God, what am I doing? Aren't I an awful person for reacting to this situation by stuffing myself full of food? I know from my *Vogue* magazines how wrong this is, and that if I get fat he will love me even less. OK, he loves Camilla, and she's fat, but I know, if I try hard, if I get it right, then "daddy" will love me again. I know what I'll do . . . I can't actually take myself away from the food; I've already eaten it. But I can throw up, and then it won't affect me.

'So Diana's case is an absolute classic. Every time something happens she feels bad about, she reacts by eating. Then she feels bad about having eaten and blames herself. And then she throws up, which solves her problem, not only on a symbolic level – she's purging herself – but also on a very realistic level, because the food doesn't pass into the stomach, and so she doesn't put on weight.'

Basically, concludes Quilliam, Diana is a food addict. Dr Lefever wholeheartedly agrees. He subscribes to the minority view that addiction is a genetic condition rather than a psychiatric one. That is to say, while it can be triggered by environmental influences, its origins are biological. His experience of treating 1400 addicts as in-patients over the past decade has persuaded him that addiction stems from a genetic shortage of dopamine-receptor genes, chemicals active in the mood centres of the brain. As a result he is unequivocal in his assertion that the only difference between food addiction and drug addiction is the substance. Sugar, he says, 'is a drug in the same way as cannabis is a drug or cocaine is a drug.'

'Eating disorders are not primarily about body weight or food,' he argues, 'it's about how you feel about yourself in the same way that alcoholism isn't primarily about alcohol, it's about how you feel about yourself. I think what happens with anorexia, for example, is that the person who is anorexic knows that if he or she starts hitting the refined carbohydrates, they won't know how to stop. Therefore it's safer not to start, and then what happens is they discover that starvation has a mood-altering effect of its own, in the same way as, if you're an alcoholic, certain behaviour has a mood-altering effect – just being in the pub and having the noise and a glass in your hand gives you a buzz.

'So there are addictive behaviours, such as gambling, work and exercise, that go along with addictive substances. There's no substance involved, but you're still stimulating your neuro-transmission systems, and the starvation involved in anorexia is mood-altering in its own right. Just as you send heroin addicts to Narcotics Anonymous, I believe it is sensible to treat other people with addictions alongside each other, so they get to know each other, so they can look across the room and see somebody else with the same type of behaviour. They may be using a different substance, but it's insight into the nature of the behaviour which is important. That's the principle on which we work.'

Dr Lefever says Diana has no prospect of an enduring recovery from her bulimia without participating in a programme of group therapy. Her visits to Susie Orbach, he claims, are simply not enough, and her illness could reoccur at any time, like any other addiction like alcoholism.

'A one-to-one arrangement will never work,' he says. 'A one-to-one with someone like me would not work. I'm not making any comment about Susie Orbach as a therapist. I'm simply saying that you can't treat addiction on a one-to-one basis because, as a patient, I can manipulate you. All I've got to do is tell you you're wonderful and look deeply into your eyes, and you're going to believe it, and then I've got you. I would never do any of my addiction work one-to-one.'

This distrust of one-to-one treatment is shared by many thera-pists who deal with people suffering from Borderline Personality Disorder. 'BPD sufferers have an uncanny knack for diagnosing – seeing through – their therapist's character,' says American therapist Gordon James, 'and for perceiving the therapist's uncertainties, foibles and hypocrisies as well as needs, hopes and virtues. They know exactly what to say or do to engage or enrage, to touch or terrify, the person who would help them – and often enough they say or do it.'

Dr Lefever's solution is for Diana to enter a 12-step programme of group therapy with an organization like Bulimics Anonymous or Addictions Anonymous. This demands rigorously honest self-examination and a willingness to change. She would be obliged to accept that her life had become unmanageable and that a belief in a power greater than herself would help restore her to sanity. She would choose a fellow addict as a sponsor – someone in whom she would be encouraged to confide her fears and anxieties. And she would be encouraged to make a list of people she feels she has wronged in some way and make personal amends to them either verbally or in writing. Finally, she would be taught that helping other addicts is the very cornerstone of her own recovery, and it would be suggested that she take one or more of her fellow addicts under her wing as 'sponsees'.

One obvious hurdle standing in the way of treatment of this sort is Diana's huge celebrity. While all participants adhere to a strict code of secrecy regarding the identity of fellow members and what they divulge in meetings, there would inevitably be high-level concern that such a senior member of the Royal Family was opening her heart to outsiders.

Dr Lefever does not see this as a problem, however. 'Now imagine trying to be in recovery if you're an international figure,' he says. 'How do you do that? Famous alcoholics can go to a London meeting on Sunday mornings popularly known as Stars on Sunday, for example. That's where Sir Anthony Hopkins and Eric Clapton go, and it's known that they go, like you might go to evening classes in typing. Who gives a toss? It doesn't make any difference if you're a star, and a princess could go just the same. If, for example, she was to speak about something in an anonymous fellowship meeting there are plenty of things she could say about how she feels that are considerably less damaging to herself than the things she's already said publicly.'

So why doesn't she go? 'The same reason that I wouldn't go,' he says, 'the same reason that you wouldn't go, the same reason that somebody who's completely unknown wouldn't go, we don't want to get better. Our addictive disease is an internal spiritual parasite. It's like Alien, it's in there, and it governs what we see, what we hear, what we say. What we have to do in treatment is to help people separate themselves from the disease, to see that they've got an internal spiritual parasite that is driving them, but it's not them. We have to help them with the shame of being an addict as well as the guilt of the things they've done.'

If Diana went to Lefever, he would tell her: 'I'm not remotely ashamed of being an addict, and I'm not remotely proud of being in recovery. It is simply what I do. I never, never, never want to go back into the pain, the lowliness, the emptiness of my addiction. I'm not going back there, and for that reason I stay going to the anonymous fellowship meetings. I stay reaching out to help newcomers. I stay abstinent from mood-altering substances and processes that might affect me simply because I've had enough pain. I don't want to go back there. I think Susie Orbach has probably done a wonderful job in comforting her, helping her, supporting her, but I don't think it's going to help her addictive behaviour.'

A refusal to tackle her addiction through group therapy could have dire consequences, according to Dr Lefever. 'It will progress,' he says. 'We get older, and we're on a helter-skelter. My addiction got progressively worse. By the time I reached 47, which is when I got into recovery, I was in a lot of trouble. I was in big trouble with an eating disorder. I was in big trouble with my gambling. It's progressive, and, if you don't get into recovery, it's going to get worse.'

Asked how serious he considers Diana's condition, Dr Lefever replies: 'God, it's bad enough.' He goes on: 'I think what we have to do is look at the consequences of it in her life. How bad does anybody's life become? You don't have to see the elephant, you can see where the elephant's been.' He argues that Diana's problems are similar to those suffered by many addicts and concludes, 'she's manifestly in trouble.'

However, Dr Lefever's most startling finding, based on his years of research, is that there is a strong statistical link between bulimia and sexual abuse in childhood, abuse that might comprise an isolated incident at the hands of a complete stranger or more regular victimization by a neighbour or a family member.

'Everyone has these fanciful notions that bulimia is vomiting out the semen as a result of sexual abuse in early childhood,' he says. 'Thousands of girls get sexually abused in childhood, and they don't all become bulimic, so you can't make that connection. However, if you see girls who are bulimic, the vast majority of them have been sexually abused in childhood. Some 90 per cent or more have been sexually abused as a child, but it isn't the sexual abuse which causes it. It's the genetic inheritance that causes it, and it's the sexual abuse that triggers it. That's what explains the fact that you can get vast numbers of people who are sexually abused who don't become addicted in one way or another.'

Dr Lefever, who charges £1750 a week for in-patient treatment at his internationally renowned recovery centre, concludes this point with the following remarkable exchange in a tape-recorded interview with the authors:

HUTCHINS AND MIDGLEY: 'Ninety per cent were sexually abused? So there's a very good chance that Diana was sexually abused as a young girl?'

LEFEVER: 'Very good chance. Very high chance. Bear in mind that I'm only talking percentages, I'm not talking specifics, I'm not talking about a patient that I've ever met.'

While Diana has never indicated that she suffered sexual abuse in childhood, the statistical link between it and bulimia is supported by the American academic Jeffrey Masson. A former dyed-in-the-wool Freudian, he turned on the psychoanalytic community largely as a result of its refusal to recognize widespread sexual abuse as a reality rather than the product of Freudian fantasy.

Of the 90 per cent statistic quoted by Dr Lefever, he says: 'I think that that's not at all impossible. Bulimia is something that has a great deal to do with one's sexual image, and the sexual image is basically destroyed by an early sexual experience. That's the problem. There's no doubt now that early experiences that are not consensual like that are very damaging in later life for the person. They cause things like bulimia, they cause things like so-called neurosis and even psychosis.'

Another US-based expert, Dr Preston Zucker, associate professor of paediatrics at the Albert Einstein College of Medicine in New York, says there is some dispute over the extent of the link, however. 'There is a lot of association with sexual abuse in childhood,' he says, 'but there is controversy over whether that's true or not because there's also an association with depression, obsessive compulsive disorder and personality disturbances. So whether that just means that a patient who has lot of psychiatric problems may also have bulimia as a problem, or whether there is a specific cause is a difficult question to answer.'

It would appear, however, that when bulimia is accompanied by deliberate self-harm, the correlation with sexual abuse is even more marked. Professor Hubert Lacey's work with multi-impulsive bulimics – those who, like Diana, also cut themselves – leads him to conclude that self-cutting is mainly done at a time of emotional stress. 'Many had been sexually abused so they cut the parts of their body they could not bear because of their sexual significance,' he told *Cosmopolitan* magazine. 'The thighs and forearms were the most common sites, although some attack their upper arms, stomach and breasts. They look for areas that are easy to get at but can be covered up.'

Everyone in Professor Lacey's sample said they hated their bodies: 82 per cent attacked the part of the body they hated most or the one that brought them the most unwarranted sexual attention; 72 per cent cut themselves because draining blood acted as a form of tranquillizer. 'They felt sedated in the same way you might feel calm after drinking alcohol, taking certain drugs or eating a lot of food,' he said. 'This is probably due to the release of endorphins, substances that have a similar chemical structure to morphine.'

Masson has no doubts of the association between bulimia and self-mutilation. 'The two things are linked,' he says. 'I've seen a number of articles about self-mutilation going back to something like that. I remember one case, in particular, that struck me was when they asked the young woman why she cut herself, she said, "Because then nobody can deny that that happened to me, I have the proof." When she was pushed, it turned out that what she meant by "that" was that whenever she tried to talk to anyone about what her father had done, they said, "No, it didn't happen." She had no proof of it. So here was a way. By cutting herself, she was showing "You see, this really did happen to me." I think self-mutilation is a form of a cry for help.'

It is only in recent years that the idea of widespread child sexual abuse has gained a grudging acceptance, helped by revelations from celebrities such as Roseanne Barr, who claims to have been sexually abused by her parents, and the late comedienne Marti Caine, who levelled a similar charge at her grandfather.

'I'm particularly down on psychoanalysts because, historically, they were the ones who set us back 100 years by claiming that sexual abuse never happened,' says Masson. 'Freud claimed that the women were fantasizing. This was a wish, this was part of how he discovered the Oedipus complex. When a person had a desire for the parent of the other sex, they confused the desire with reality, they think it really happened, when all it is is a fantasy that was repressed in early childhood. His claim was, "Every child wants this, and they can't bear to think about that when they hit adolescence," so, instead of thinking about the wish they had, they invent the deed. That was his position, and he was just wrong on that. What I tried to do with my first book, *Assault on Truth*, is to discover why Freud felt it necessary to take that position, I think it's because society around him would simply not permit him to believe that women were sexually abused, so he wouldn't have had a practice. He wouldn't have gotten anywhere.

'Psychoanalysts have changed in the last couple of years. I think there's been so much knowledge among the general public about sexual abuse that even the dinosaur analysts don't want to take the position that it never happens, but for many years they were. They were saying it was one in a million cases. So somebody like the Princess of Wales, who may have been sexually abused in childhood, goes [to an analyst], and they say, "Well, that's a fantasy," and, if a memory starts, they dismiss it. At least they did until recently. Susie Orbach doesn't do that, she's part of the feminist movement, and I'm sure she's more receptive to it than most people.

'I know nothing whatsoever about Princess Diana, the only point and it's one that a number of feminine therapists have made, and it's a good one, is that people who seek therapy have a higher chance of being sexually abused than the ordinary population. So today we know that approximately one in three women have been sexually abused.'

Masson explains that child sexual abuse covers a multitude of sins, from having the breasts or genitals touched to actual rape. 'It would generally be by somebody at least ten years older,' he says. 'It could be anyone. The statistic is 38 per cent [of women]. That's here in the United States, I don't think they've ever done such a survey in England, but I wouldn't imagine it would be that different.' He adds that among hospital in-patients, women psychiatrists report a figure nearer 50 per cent.

Dr Lefever's argument that bulimics are addicts is not universally shared, however. Professor Lacey's senior research lecturer, Dr

Pippa Hugo, takes issue with Dr Lefever's assertion that bulimia is an addiction in a physical sense. She does concede, though, that it might be an ongoing response to 'feelings that are otherwise intolerable'. She says: 'Some people might drink to damp down how they feel. Then, in that respect, one can view it in the same way [as an addiction]. We'd probably view bulimia as a way of coping with life, stresses, feelings and thoughts, and it might be precipitated by a number of different things. But in terms of it being addictive, no, I don't think so. It's certainly not physically addictive. I know some people recommend staying off certain foods and view it as carbohydrate sensitivity or something like that, but I don't agree with that.'

Nor is she convinced that group therapy is the only answer. 'I don't think there's necessarily that much to choose between the different kinds of treatment [one-to-one and group therapy],' she says. 'I think if you have a therapist who actually knows what she's doing, then she would not be manipulated by the patient. We have groups for our in-patients but not for our out-patients. There are advantages in groups in that people can be confronted by their peers and not just by another professional, but I think if the therapist is experienced enough, you shouldn't come across those problems. Most therapists are under supervision or have peer support from others, which helps to keep one objective, I guess.'

At St George's, Dr Hugo and her colleagues take a softly-softly approach. The use of fluoxetine and fluvoxamine, the antidepressants most commonly used to combat bulimia, are avoided in favour of diet and weight-management programmes and psychotherapy.

'The only time we might consider sectioning is where somebody who's anorexic wasn't able to make a decision about treatment because of their physical state,' says Dr Hugo. 'They might be so physically unwell that they don't really have any clear thoughts. In that sense you'd be sectioning them to keep them alive.' She adds that deaths from bulimia are extremely rare. 'I could envisage circumstances in which they might die. If their potassium level became so disordered that it affected their heart, for example, but I've never come across it. Many of these women can be very distressed and very depressed and may die, not from bulimia, but from attempts that they make on their lives, and so that's another thing to bear in mind.'

Dr Zucker says the rates for recovery from bulimia are still running below 50 per cent, and that there are no major breakthroughs on the horizon. 'The treatment for bulimia seems to be fairly fixed at using cognitive behavioural therapy,' he says. 'Most people will regard medication as an adjunct to that, which may increase the cure rate by at least a small amount. But there is a very big question about what to do with a group of patients who after cognitive behavioural therapy do not get better.'

The woman who treats Diana two or three times a week is forbidden by the ethics of her profession from discussing her case, but there are many clues to what might pass between Susie Orbach and her client in her comprehensive study of eating disorders, *Hunger Strike*, published in 1986. Orbach traces the roots of anorexia nervosa – said to be responsible for the deaths of 150,000 women a year in the United States – to the aspects of the sixties revolution that championed slimness as the ideal female form. She cites the move away from the celebration of the voluptuousness of actresses such as Marilyn Monroe, Gina Lollabrigida and Jayne Mansfield to the lauding of the sylph-like figures of 'the Shrimp' – Jean Shrimpton – and Twiggy.

'Thirty years ago,' Orbach writes, 'a young woman would not necessarily have sought a solution to low self-esteem through the transformation of her body and the drastic denial of a biological aspect of her femininity. For she would not have grown up in a culture preoccupied by the abundance of food linked with a need for girls and women to deprive themselves of it.'

Today the Shrimp has been replaced by a legion of underfed supermodels from Kate Moss to Jodie Kydd, and politicians and agony aunts regularly berate the editors of teenage magazines for their promotion of the notion that, in bodily terms, less is more.

Orbach points out that while middle-aged film star Jane Fonda has come clean about her own bulimic past, she persists with 'a similarly obsessive solution – exercise'. This observation will have great resonance for Diana. 'Strenuous exercise in increasing amounts is often central to the maintenance of a psychic balance, as is the denial of food,' Orbach declares, citing fitness regimes of 'a punishing and extraordinary nature'. She goes on: 'It is not uncommon to encounter an anorectic taking two or three "killer" exercise classes in a row or working for 40 minutes a day on the Nautilus machine after a seven-mile run.' Tellingly, she adds: 'Sadly, those efforts have to be repeated daily, and increasingly, for the person to maintain the feeling, which is transitory.' While the reference here is to anorectics rather than bulimics, it is clearly a syndrome that runs through both conditions and presents an uncannily accurate description of Diana's own obsession.

In a section of her book dealing with the problems of compatibility between therapist and client, Orbach not only advises the therapist to be sensitive to the cultural influences of a client from a younger generation – as Diana is – but also warns that 'if she [the therapist] is from a different class, she may perceive the environment as more benevolent than it in fact is to her client.' There seems little danger of Orbach overestimating the 'benevolence' of Diana's Palace background, however.

This does not stop her recommending – like Dr Lefever has done above – group therapy for bulimics, something Diana might well find hard to stomach. Orbach advocates 'themed groups' on sexuality, on the mother-daughter relationship, on jealousy, on fear and on anger. As we have seen, Diana could benefit from any one of these groups.

As her bulimia took hold, Diana was going through the emotional and physiological turmoil of her first pregnancy, and, when William was born, the initial elation was followed by a crippling bout of post-natal depression. 'It had been quite a difficult pregnancy,' she said. 'I hadn't been very well throughout it so, by the time William arrived, it was a great relief because it was all peaceful again, and I was well for a time. Then I was unwell with post-natal depression, which no one ever discusses, you have to read about it afterwards, and that in itself was a bit of a difficult time. You'd wake up in the morning feeling you didn't want to get out of bed, you felt misunderstood, and just very very low in yourself.' She claimed this was completely out of character. 'I never had a depression in my life,' she said. 'But then, when I analysed it, I could see that the changes

I'd made in the last year had all caught up with me and my body had said, "We want a rest."'

What Churchill called 'the black dog of despair' was no stranger to Diana and her family. Her favourite uncle, Edmund Fermoy, the man who had vouched for her virginity at the time of her engagement, ended a long period of depression by shooting himself in the stables of his 700-acre estate in 1984. Her father, Earl Spencer, was said to have been prone to 'maudlin self-pity' and sudden rages.

The Royal Family, however, takes a dim view of what it apparently sees as self-indulgent weakness. Asked on *Panorama* how they had reacted to her post-natal depression, Diana replied: 'Well, maybe I was the first person ever to be in this family who ever had a depression or was ever openly tearful. And obviously that was daunting, because if you've never seen it before, how do you support it?'

Her in-laws' predictable reaction – 'Diana's unstable and Diana's mentally unbalanced – would have been a harsh judgement, according to psychologist Dr David Nias. 'If that's true, it was unfair,' he says. 'The Royal Family should have had expert opinion. It could have been explained to her that post-natal depression is something that comes out of the blue and is not her fault in any way. It is a temporary biochemical disturbance. I was amazed by what she was saying on *Panorama* about not having support.'

Post-natal depression is now a well-established reaction to giving birth among a large number of women. There are two basic types: psychotic and neurotic. 'The worrying type is the psychotic one,' says Dr Nias. 'In these cases, the mother becomes psychotic and has thoughts of killing the child. It's a temporary insanity. The mother just doesn't feel worthy of giving birth and feels it would be better for the world if she and her child disappeared. The more neurotic type just feels terribly low and experiences a sense of terrible anti-climax, and then she starts feeling guilty because she's not looking after the baby properly. That's when the mother will need help. These days it's treated almost entirely with medication. In the old days psychoanalysis was used, but now it's antidepressant drugs, variations on Prozac.'

Psychotic cases are rare, and so, statistically, it's almost certain that she had the neurotic one, which quite a lot of women do suffer from. Often it goes undiagnosed, the family say, "Oh, well, she'll get over it," but that's like ignoring pain, saying it's natural. That's silly when there's treatment available. If it's treated, it will last for two or three weeks, but untreated it will go on for several months. Once a mother gets on a real down, it's self-perpetuating.'

It would seem, however, that Diana's depression preceded the birth of William. She was nervous and weepy during her pregnancy, and psychotherapists and psychologists who treated her at this time suggested antidepressants. As her depression persisted, Diana's inner struggles grew, and she took to self-mutilation.

'When no one listens to you, or you feel no one's listening to you, all sorts of things start to happen,' she confessed. 'For instance, you have so much pain inside yourself that you try and hurt yourself on the outside because you want help, but it's the wrong help you're asking for. People see it as crying wolf or attention-seeking, and they think because you are in the media all the time you've got enough attention, inverted commas. But I was actually crying out, because I wanted to get better in order to go forward and continue my duty and my role as wife, mother, Princess of Wales. So, yes, I did inflict upon myself. I didn't like myself, I was ashamed because I couldn't cope with the pressures.'

Asked to be specific about the injury she caused herself, Diana replied: 'Well, I just hurt my arms and legs, and I work in environments now when I see women doing similar things, and I'm able to understand completely where they are coming from.'

She went on to admit that many of the incidents took place in her husband's presence. 'Well, I didn't actually always do it in front of him,' she said. 'But obviously anyone who loves someone would be very concerned about it.' And in a telling response to the question 'Did he understand what was behind the physical act of hurting yourself do you think?', she said: 'No, but not many people would have taken the time to see that.'

One person who can strongly identify with what Diana was going through is Diane Harrison, author of *Vicious Circle*, who also developed bulimia during her teenage years and took refuge in self-mutilation. She says Diana's habit of cutting herself in front of her husband is most unusual. 'I see it as being a form of non-verbal communication,' she says. 'If you're trying to put a point across to someone, and they're clearly not listening, then you may go and cut yourself. It's like, you know, "This is how I feel. I'm really angry with you." There's a lot of anger surrounding it, and unspoken feelings that, in Diana's case, maybe she was unable to get across. It's mostly done in secret. There's almost a ritual to it. Some people begin by cutting themselves less severely, but if their feelings are not relieved through it they may begin cutting more severely. It's kind of a release for feelings. The sensation can be soothing.'

Dr Eric Shepherd agrees that at the root of Diana's dramatic display of hurt was probably her inability to elicit any reaction from her husband. 'If you get to a point where it seems as though your trying to hurt the other person doesn't work,' he says, 'or if the other person doesn't even take any notice of your entreaties to listen to you, to love you or whatever, then it's very common for people to harm themselves. You'd be surprised at how much self-mutilation goes on.'

The seriousness of the cutting varies widely. The most extreme cases can cut themselves so severely that they lose as much as a litre of blood at a time, and the wounds require stitches. Sufferers use anything from razors and shards of glass to kitchen knives. Diana, who admitted to cutting her arms and legs, restricted herself to relatively superficial cuts, however. But the consequences were alarming nonetheless. On one particularly dramatic occasion after a heated row with Charles over whether she would join him on holiday at Balmoral, she disappeared into the lavatory of the plane carrying them from RAF Northolt to Swansea. When she finally emerged, there was blood trickling down her arms, and she proceeded to smear it along the walls of the aircraft of the Queen's Flight.

However distressing this incident might have been, it was clearly not a serious attempt on her life, and Harrison insists that self-cutting is not based on a desire to end it all. 'It's a coping mechanism,' she says. 'It's not about trying to die, it's about trying to stay alive; trying to express what you can't in any other way. If you never managed to get those feelings out you might become so depressed that taking your own life felt like the only way out, but that's much further along the way.'

Dr Dennis Friedman agrees. He reckons it was mistaken inter-
pretations of her self-cutting episodes that led to sensational
allegations that she had tried to kill herself. 'Those suicide attempts
in the past weren't exactly suicide attempts, they were what's called
parasuicide, a kind of cry for help,' he says. 'When she cut her wrist
it wasn't a great big cut that would cause her to bleed to death, they
were tiny little cuts. These are not things that are to do with wanting
to end one's life. They are saying, "Look, I am suffering. You must
help me. I'm in pain."'

It is a very serious, if widespread, condition, nevertheless, says
Dr Dorothy Rowe: 'Women who cut themselves – and I've spent a
lot of time listening to them – describe two things: intense tension
and intense self-hatred. So you cut yourself. The immediate pain
relieves the tension, and it's also punishing yourself.' She argues that
hating oneself is part and parcel of being depressed. 'With post-
natal depression, the woman feels that she just can't cope with her
situation; she blames herself, feels inadequate and feels that she's
not being given support and reassurance by other people,' she says.
'Yes, that would make her feel that she was a bad mother.'

Just as she claims to have shaken off her bulimia – 'I'm free of
it now' – Diana says she no longer cuts herself. Quite what
treatment she received is unclear, but, in the most serious cases, the
measures used are quite draconian.

'People see self-mutilation as crying wolf or attention-seeking,
which it isn't, because it's a recognized syndrome, a diagnostic
category,' says Dr Nias. 'One of my earliest cases involved a 17 year
old girl who had to be kept in a padded cell although she was
perfectly normal in all other respects. She would say to me, "I just
don't know why I do this." If she could get to a light bulb, she
would break it and cut herself with it. It's like a compulsion. She
couldn't explain it, and neither could her doctors. The recommended treatment, the latest treatment for that condition, is
learning theory. A patient is rewarded for not hurting herself, and
you find some way of punishing her for doing it. One of the forms
of punishment is electric shocks. You zap them every time they go
to do it. They do it for head-banging too, which is a sub-category of
self-mutilation.'

Asked if he would have recommended electric-shock treatment

for the Princess if she were a serious case, he says: 'Yes, that would be part of it. The emphasis would be on rewarding her for not doing it through affection, social attention, somebody cheerfully talking to her. You condition the patient to change their priorities so that they would naturally do things that would bring reward as a habit. It's a straightforward learning theory.

'The electric-shock method works in theory but is rarely used in practice because of the ethical and practical problems. There's no evidence that talking is sufficiently powerful to help anybody, it just makes them feel better at the time.'

The exact nature of the treatment Diana received for the very serious illness from which she has suffered has never been made clear. When she was given an opportunity to go into the detail of the help she was given for her post-natal depression during the *Panorama* interview, she would only say, 'I received a great deal of treatment.' Given her wilful reputation and the underdeveloped nature of many of the treatments available to combat bulimia and self-mutilation, there must be serious doubt over how lasting her recovery will be.

ELEVEN

THE FLORENCE NIGHTINGALE SYNDROME

'Someone's got to go out there and love people and show it.'

THE PRINCESS OF WALES

Wearing a gown of surgical blue, matching head scarf and a regulation face mask, she watched intently as one of the world's most respected specialists performed open-heart surgery on a seven-year-old boy. But subtle aspects of her appearance marked her out from the rest of the theatre team. While they had all pushed every strand of hair under their surgical caps, scrubbed their faces clean of make-up and removed their jewellery in the interests of maintaining a sterile environment, the tall woman who glanced occasionally into the lens of the television cameras that rarely left her face had made fewer concessions to good medical practice.

Princess Diana was on stage. For her this was not just an operating theatre. A tuft of blonde hair peeped attractively from beneath her head covering, her eyes were enhanced by liberal applications of eyeliner and mascara, and the camera lights glinted on a pair of circular gold ear-rings. The would-be Queen of people's hearts was taking herself at her word. It was the sixth heart operation she had witnessed, and only the previous week she had observed a woman suffering from breast cancer having a mastectomy.

She justified this exercise in surgical voyeurism by saying: 'It is literally seeing life on the knife-edge. It motivates me. It brings purpose and meaning to my life.' It undoubtedly bought valuable publicity to Harefield Hospital and the charity Chain of Hope, which organized the operation for a boy from Cameroon. But, most of all, it served as a fix to satisfy Diana's addiction to publicity. Sky TV gave the royal visit extensive coverage on its evening news show, and the newspapers were full of it the next day.

It was clear that this was a mercy mission too far, however. So frequent had Diana's visits to the sick become that people were beginning to joke about carrying cards saying they did not want to be visited by her in hospital. The Harefield affair was immediately branded a 'stunt', and it was hard to see how even her most devoted fans could not construe it as involving an element of photo opportunity. Agony aunt Claire Rayner, a former theatre sister herself, was widely quoted on the hygiene risks associated with having an unnecessary extra person around the operating table.

'I don't care who it was who went into that theatre, no lay person who has no real business there should be allowed in,' she says. 'Everybody who comes into an operating theatre brings his or her own supply of micro-organisms.'

Others saw it as further evidence that the Princess was becoming increasingly unhinged. 'It really is quite incredible,' says image consultant Mary Spillane. 'Quite frankly, I think she is all over the place, and this interest that she has in medicine, to the point of standing in on open-heart surgery, is bizarre to say the least, and so is the fact that she recognized it as a photo opportunity, and they let her do it.

'It obviously was a publicity stunt, because they would not have been able to either film it with her being there or release the pictures and photographs without her permission. It's all part of the image she thinks she wants to project.

'The make-up was very heavy, and it just shows that she is very hung up about the way she looks, despite what she says. She's always complaining about the media, saying things like: "All they do is comment about my hairstyle or my latest dress," you know, "Poor me, that's all I'm known for, when I'm really a serious person." If she was a serious person, first of all she wouldn't have allowed the filming in there, she would have kept it quiet. Then, she would have

Under Pressure
(above): While few have courted publicity more than Diana, there were times when the constant pressure of photographers got to her. (ALPHA)

Entertaining Miss Sloane (right): Diana leaving San Lorenzo, the Belgravia set's favourite restaurant, where she lunched Oliver Hoare and other men friends. (ALPHA)

Slick Opera
(previous pages): A fashionable Princess opted for a radically different hairstyle at an awards ceremony in New York.
(CAMERA PRESS)

Now You See Her...
(below): Stepping out of the Harbour Club in Fulham on a day when she was happy to display her legs to the photographers who assemble each morning to record her comings and goings. (ALPHA)

... Now You Don't
(left): The day after it was repo... she had cellui... a wore a full ... her ... fac... ph... hope of a... pictures b... published. In the event her eccentric exit received blanket coverage. (BRENDAN BEIRNE, REX FEATURES)

All the Fun of the Fair (above): Diana fostered her image as a caring mother by tipping off photographers the day before she took her sons to Thorpe Park. (REX FEATURES)

Day Tripper (right): At the height of her unhappiness, Diana made a solo trip to Benidorm. She stayed for only 18 hours at a tourist hotel before flying home to her palace. (DAVE DYSON, CAMERA PRESS)

Distant Majesty (above): The Queen is one of the few who have remained consistently immune to the Princess's charms. (REX FEATURES)

Mad Hatters (below): Diana's friendship with Sarah, Duchess of York known to the world as Fergie, is one of the few that has endured. The Princess has never felt threatened by her tarnished sister-in-law and their association has survived a series of ructions. (KEN GOFF, CAMERA PRESS)

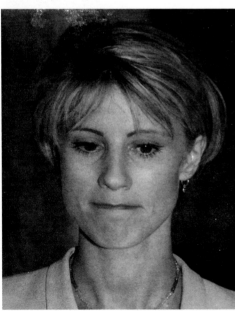

Good Sport (right):
England rugby captain
Will Carling paid one
too many visits to
Diana's Kensington

Palace apartment for
his wife's liking. Julia
Carling (above) sued
for divorce.

(BOTH REX FEATURES)

Lady's Man (left): Captain James Hewitt, the man who pulled off the ultimate kiss and tell. (ALPHA)

Nanny Knows Best (below): Diana resents Alexandra 'Tiggy' Legge-Bourke's growing influence over her children. Prince William, in particular, enjoys her company. (ALPHA)

Coffee Mate (below): Christopher Whalley, the man who formed a close friendship with Diana after she invited him to buy her a coffee at their gym. (TIM ROOKE, REX FEATURES)

Back Seat Driver (above): Charles's mistress, Camilla Parker Bowles, the woman who looks set to be the power behind the throne if and when her lover becomes king. (REX FEATURES)

Driving Miss Crazy (above): Soon after he left Diana's employ, chauffeur Steve Davies incurred her displeasure by spending the night with her dresser at Kensington Palace. (REX FEATURES)

Shink Rapt (right): The Princess of Wales made regular visits to the north London home of psychotherapist Susie Orbach. (ALPHA)

been, like everyone else there, well scrubbed. She was in absolute full make-up, and Diana bizarre make-up, at that, with the full black eyeliner that she thinks makes her look very serious, and all the rest of it. So you get another example of the extremes that she will go to to try and cultivate her own image.

'She's now supposed to be getting professional advice, but it's very bizarre advice. It all seems as if she really is manipulating things behind the scenes. She isn't the victim she sets herself up to be, this was quite an orchestrated thing.'

So why did the Princess lay herself open to such damning criticism? The problem on this particular occasion, according to *Sun* editor Stuart Higgins, may have been that her press advisor, Jane Atkinson, did not even know that the visit was going ahead. The day it happened she was thousands of miles away in Chicago setting up a trip for Diana to a hospital there.

Lord Archer takes the charitable view. 'There are going to be misjudgements because she's making ten decisions a week, and, like the Prime Minister, a minister or a shadow minister,' he says, 'we all make mistakes.'

A less charitable view is that she felt the need to crank up her profile at a time when she was being put in the shade by other royals, or even that her preoccupation with watching operations is part of yet another macabre syndrome. On the publicity front she had been losing out to both the Queen – whose seventieth birthday celebrations were in full swing – and her sister-in-law, the Duchess of York, whose divorce was grabbing the headlines. Diana the media junky may well have been suffering withdrawal symptoms.

As one psychotherapist puts it: 'The person who does not have a strong self-identity, whose ego is so frail that they almost feel they do not exist unless the outside world is giving them attention and feedback, will resort to desperate measures to get the attention they need. Without it they can literally feel they are disintegrating.'

More intriguingly the Princess is not the only figure to have a morbid fascination with the manipulation of the surgeon's knife. Noël Coward, the playwright and entertainer, developed a similar preoccupation after falling ill with a blood disorder while appearing in cabaret in Las Vegas in the fifties. The renowned specialist who treated him subsequently invited his star patient to observe an

operation in a hospital in Chicago. Coward, enthralled by proce-
dures that were then seen as being at the cutting-edge of medical
science, developed a fascination for this macabre spectator sport
and sat in on several more.

'In the old days people used to go to public executions, so in a
way it might be equivalent to that,' says Dr David Nias, 'a deep-
seated psychological need to witness life and death in the balance.
In evolutionary theory terms people who have got that sort of fascination may, in a way, be better prepared when their lives are in
danger, because they'll be cool, calm and collected because they're
used to that drama. Whereas if you were witnessing that for the first
time, you'd panic; therefore you wouldn't survive, you wouldn't
have children, and so you wouldn't pass on this tendency using the
Darwinian [survival of the fittest] analogy. So there's good reason to
be fascinated by surgery.

'In a violent world, if we take an interest in these things, we
desensitize ourselves so that in a crisis situation we don't panic. Just
like to be a soldier you have to learn to kill without your hand
shaking. The more you take an interest in life-and-death situations,
the more prepared you are, so it is part of our psyche that has
evolved, and some people really are fascinated by it.'

For those who are not convinced by such a theory, American
academic Jeffrey Masson proposes another. 'I wouldn't be surprised
if somebody came to me and told me, "You know, I don't understand why, but I just have to go into hospitals,"' he says. 'My first
thought would be that something had happened to her for which
she was hospitalized, and about which she was never told. That's
exactly the kind of thing where an unconscious memory can be the
motor for the behaviour. It wouldn't surprise me to learn that what
she discusses with Susie Orbach is something about an early
operation that she was never told about. It's very common,
especially in England, that children are operated on and not told, in
the hope that they will forget it, and, of course, it doesn't work. It
just compels them to do certain things, and they don't understand
why, so my theory would be that something happened to her that
involved surgery.'

• • •

Whatever her motives the Princess obviously cannot get enough of this kind of thing. One man who can give us some insight into what form her visits take is Joseph Toffolo, husband of her acupuncturist, Oonagh. At the age of 70 the retired architect had just had a triple heart by-pass and valve-repair operation, and he was lying in a west London hospital, critically ill. Diana knew that his wife was desperately concerned about him.

Ultimately Diana paid well over a dozen visits to his bedside during his 18-day hospitalization. On each occasion she arrived laden with presents. There were grapes, books, flowers and records by her friend Luciano Pavarotti, the world-famous tenor. But the gift she obviously considered most precious of all was herself. Far from finding this a traumatic and draining process, Diana drew strength from the elderly patient's appreciation.

'I felt compelled to perform,' she told *Panorama*. 'Well, when I say perform, I was compelled to go out and do my engagements and not let people down and support them and love them. And, in a way, by being out in public, they supported me although they weren't aware just how much healing they were giving me, and it carried me through.'

As Dr Dorothy Rowe explains: 'If you've been sitting around a palace doing absolutely nothing all day, and you've been waited on hand and foot, and then you just go out and enjoy yourself, as nice as that is, it doesn't feel as if you are actually getting something done. So you go to a hospital and see some people who are sick, and the smiles on their faces say to you, You've made me feel better. Then you feel, I haven't entirely wasted my time, I've achieved something. Ultimately no one ever does anything entirely altruistically.'

To the bemusement of staff and patient alike, Kensington's answer to Mother Teresa would stay for long periods and even then appear reluctant to leave.

'It all rather surprised me, I must admit,' says Joe Toffolo, who barely knew his wife's illustrious client. 'You expect to see her once, perhaps, but not so many times. I'm not quite sure what she was up to.'

There was a time when Diana herself hadn't known. Two months after those visits to Joe Toffolo's bedside, she told *Panorama* that when she became a working royal she had to create her own niche: 'No one sat me down with a piece of paper and said, "This is what is expected of you." But, there again, I'm lucky enough in the fact that I have found my role, and I am very conscious of it, and I love being with people.' She added: 'I remember when I used to sit on hospital beds and hold people's hands, people used to be sort of shocked because they said they had never seen this before, and, to me, it was quite a normal thing to do. And when I saw the reassurance that an action like that gave, I did it everywhere and will always do that.'

No one can deny the consolation provided by these visits to the sick and the dying, to hostels for the homeless and to sanctuaries for battered wives. But what is equally undeniable is the enormous public-relations boost that such apparently selfless activities bring her. For, on many of her visits, she is accompanied by a pack of photographers and reporters, eager for pictures and stories to satisfy the insatiable public demand for news of their fairytale princess.

This, however, does not tell the whole story. Her preoccupation with those less fortunate than herself dates back to her days at West Heath school. There headmistress Miss Rudge championed acts of 'good citizenship' among her girls, encouraging them to visit the old and the sick in the vicinity. As a result, Diana and a friend would make weekly visits to an elderly lady in nearby Sevenoaks, where they would chat over tea and help with the housework. She also got involved with mentally and physically handicapped patients at a local mental hospital and worked with hyperactive youngsters.

Years later she paid a visit to her old home on the Sandringham Estate, Park House, which had since been turned into a Leonard Cheshire Home, and stayed for an hour and a half. 'It was just so exciting,' she told James Gilbey during their notorious Squidgygate conversation. 'They were so sweet, they had their photographs taken with me. And they kept hugging me, and they were so ill some of them. No legs, you know, and all sorts of things.'

Gilbey, showing uncharacteristic powers of perception, ignored the detail and immediately homed in on the adulation aspect. 'You can always sense a camera,' he said. 'I think you can sniff a camera at a thousand yards.' To this day, for every staged photo opportunity there is a clandestine visit in the watches of the night that passes unnoticed by the paparazzi. Perhaps, unconsciously, Diana's motives go beyond a wish to do good. To explain all this we must delve further into the mind of a highly complex personality.

On the surface her motives could not be more pure. Here we have a woman of noble birth, with every material comfort that the modern world can provide, doing what she can for the underprivileged. The truth, however, is far more complicated. As Shakespeare wrote, 'The quality of mercy is not strain'd.' It is, he said, 'twice bless'd; It blesseth him that gives and him that takes.' This is certainly the case with Diana. Experiencing increasing coldness at home, she has learned to rely for warmth on the admiration of an adoring public. In her visits to the sick she found a measure of emotional salvation and psychological recovery.

Psychologist Susan Quilliam reckons her behaviour is part of an ongoing campaign to maintain her self-esteem. 'If Diana leapt into a burning building to save a child, on some level that would be self-motivated because what would have been motivating her is the thought, I will feel good about myself when I rescue this child. But everything everyone does has some sort of spin-off for ourselves, and I say that, not to put Diana down, because we all do it. We don't do a single kind act without thinking, Oh, yes, I feel good about myself. When people come into psychotherapy they start by saying, "What I've done here is bad," and, "What I've done here is good,"' she says. 'It comes as a surprise to such people when they learn that every single action is self-motivated. Otherwise we wouldn't have martyrs. So the question for me is: how much of Diana's action is self-gratification and how much of it is *manipulative* self-gratification?

'Every human being is involved in the job of recovering from childhood problems and trying to make themselves feel good about themselves, to build self-esteem. Diana's motivation, at bottom, is almost certainly that by helping others who are less fortunate than herself she makes herself feel good about herself.

'Visiting hospitals is a very clear way of making her feel good about herself, which is ratified by society. I mean, everybody knows that visiting the sick is good, particularly if you're a princess. You are a role model. You are going to make other people feel the same way. You're going to bring kudos to the hospital. She did a lot for AIDS patients. Hugging AIDS patients did actually make a difference, because it put a message across. So that's one way Diana can feel good about herself, and she can do it justifiably.

'She probably gets a lot out of talking to other people and listening to them. I believe that she is actually a good listener, and she does actually make people feel better about themselves, that she does have a high social competence when she's talking to ordinary people.' But like many remedies, this 'compulsive helping' has serious side-effects. While her hospital visits have been described as her way of escaping her self-obsession, they are, in fact, fuelling it.

Dr Sidney Crown has no doubts on this score. 'I had a psychotherapy patient who was a solicitor in the City,' he says. 'At the end of her therapy she actually went out to join Mother Teresa and sent me reports from year to year. She is terribly happy with her work. It's not an act. Diana's much more comfortable when she is going to old folks' homes and places where you don't have to do very much really except shake hands or kiss somebody, or whatever.'

Her role as a flag-bearer for the sick and needy began to take shape in April 1987, when she opened the country's first purpose-built ward for AIDS patients at the Middlesex Hospital in London. It proved a turning-point in her life. She admits that, until she carved out her role as a sort of latter-day Florence Nightingale, she was unsure about what her public function would be.

'I was very confused about which area I should go into,' she told *Panorama*. 'Then I found myself being more and more involved with people who were rejected by society – with, I'd say, drug addicts, alcoholism, battered this, battered that – and I found an affinity here. And I respected very much the honesty I found on that level with people I met, because in hospices, for instance, when people are dying they are much more open and more vulnerable, and much more real than other people. And I appreciated that.'

Early on she championed the cause of AIDS victims, visiting wards up and down the country and making speeches. Some of the biggest names in showbusiness were rallying to the cause, keen to highlight the ravages of a disease that had claimed the lives of so many of their friends. While she might have seen it as an opportunity for involvement in a high-profile cause and ensure that she would be one of the main attractions at a series of star-studded fund-raising events, the Queen's advisors referred to it as the 'gay plague' and said it was an 'inappropriate' cause for her to adopt.

Ignoring the objections of the Palace hierarchy, Diana became patron of the National AIDS Trust after seeing babies born to HIV-positive mothers in New York. And even before she was prepared to go into the true nature of the illness, she encouraged the young Princes to share her interest in the sufferers.

'I've taken William and Harry to see people dying of AIDS,' she admits, 'albeit I told them it was cancer. I've taken the children to all sorts of areas where I'm not sure anyone of that age, in this family, has been before. And they have a knowledge. They may never use it, but the seed is there, and I hope it will grow because knowledge is power.'

Her detractors at the Palace were forced to retreat when the disease touched her own life with the death, in August 1991, of her friend Adrian Ward-Jackson, a former governor of the Royal Ballet. In his final days Diana spent a total of 22 hours at his bedside, reciting the Lord's Prayer with another friend, Angela Serota, as he drifted in and out of consciousness. He died one night at 1 am, and she remained a further seven hours to console his grieving family. In a subsequent letter to Serota, she wrote: 'My view of life has taken another direction and has become more positive and balanced.'

This moving vigil aside, other aspects of her work with AIDS patients were seen as little more than press jamborees. On one occasion headlines were ensured when she embraced an AIDS patient.

'Kissing someone with AIDS is no big deal,' says Dr Sidney Crown. 'You're not going to catch anything, to put it at its lowest. It's a gesture really and, I think, a horribly condescending gesture actually. It fills me with horror that she has to do these things. But she sees it differently. She sees it as a caring image that people rate highly in her at a time when she feels so crucified.'

But AIDS sufferers were not the only ones to get the Diana treatment. 'I understand people's suffering, people's pain more than you will ever know,' she once told the Bishop of Norwich. 'It's not only AIDS, it's anyone who suffers.' The good bishop possibly considered this a rather complacent attitude. 'He kept saying to me, "One must never think how good one is at one's job. There is always something to learn at the next corner,"' Diana told James Gilbey during their Squidgygate chat. 'And I said, "Well, people who know me know I'm not like that."'

So, like other members of the Royal Family, she threw herself into work for a variety of other good causes, including the Great Ormond Street Children's Hospital and the Royal Marsden in London, Help the Aged, the homeless project Centrepoint and Dr Barnardo's Homes. But it was her work with Birthright, now renamed WellBeing, that predated all these. She became patron of the health research charity for women and babies in 1984, when she was pregnant with Harry. It was typical of a certain type of good cause that attracts a disproportionate number of well-heeled society women, disparagingly known as 'ladies who lunch'. Lists of committee members would read like a run-down of the organizers of a debutantes' ball.

As the consorts of wealthy and powerful men, they had certain experiences in common. Their marriages often involved long periods of separation as their husbands travelled on business. In this context working for charity was a socially acceptable but unthreatening way of maintaining their self-worth without the pressures and obligations of a 'proper job'.

'Diana's comments during her *Panorama* interview about competitive undercurrents to her relationship with Charles would appear to underline the conflict women like her find themselves in,' Dr Raj Persaud, consultant psychiatrist at the Maudsley Hospital in south London, wrote in the *Daily Mail*. 'Their charisma and dedication is often in danger of stealing attention away from their husbands, so charitable work helps them achieve a balancing act of gaining social prominence but with work that can be dismissed by the ruthlessly ambitious all around them as "only for charity".'

As the young Princess grew in confidence and became more poised in public, however, the sort of group activity represented by her work for Birthright was replaced by exercises in glorious isolation.

'The most worrying aspect of Diana's recent attempts to help others is her need to do this work alone,' wrote Dr Persaud. 'Either the emotions involved agitate her so much that she needs to be alone or, for reasons of personality difficulty, she is simply unable to cooperate with others to organize help as part of any coordinated activity. This is worrying because the kind of work she is attempting to do now, while worthwhile, is also emotionally exhausting, and she will undoubtedly need support if she is to continue with it.

'Close therapeutic contact with these patients generates strong emotions, which usually need to be shared and cannot be shouldered by anyone alone. Otherwise, Diana's drive back to Kensington Palace in the early morning will, over time, become lonelier and lonelier. But, on *Panorama*, Diana repeatedly said that, despite all the problems she has faced, she is strong and gains strength from working with the sick and needy.... She seems to see strength arising from people who suffer. But one thing seems clear, after first her interview and now her hospital visits, she simply wants to be wanted.'

Dr Persaud suggests that so many of her visits are made in the middle of the night not just to avoid press attention but also because these are the times when she feels loneliest. In December 1995, for example, Diana was in regular contact with staff at two London hospitals and would make regular night-time visits to the bedsides of seriously ill patients.

'There are hundreds of patients who are there without their own loved ones, and they need a human presence,' she said. 'I really love helping, I seem to draw strength from them. I love to help, but it's just the hours I have to keep at the moment are a little crazy. I can't go during the day because it would draw too much attention to the hospitals concerned. All the patients need someone, and I love doing it, I really love doing it. I hold their hands, talk to them, tell them that everyone is on their side, whatever helps.'

Diana is adept at switching personas with dramatic effect. A good case in point was the day in July 1994, when she played Mother Teresa to the impoverished tenants of the Ely housing estate in Cardiff in the afternoon and then transformed herself into the glittering princess to party that evening among the cream of the international jetset at Tiffany's the jewellers on Bond Street, London's most chic thoroughfare. She had dressed down for the visit to Wales to open a new playground on the run-down estate, which had seen a local man murdered by vandals just days previously. There she displayed all the qualities of charm and sympathy that had won her such a huge following among ordinary people.

When she arrived in Mayfair just a few hours later, however, the man in the street was safely behind a barrier, and she barely glanced at her public as she swept majestically through the pillared entrance to mingle with the rich and titled. She was resplendent in a figure-hugging dress with a scooped neckline that showed off a magnificent sapphire the size of a quail's egg, surrounded by diamonds, and clasped to her throat by a seven-strand pearl choker. The star-struck guests were led into a curtained-off area, two-by-two, to have their heads patted by the most cosseted woman in the world.

In a life of such contrasts errors of judgement are easily made, according to clinical psychologist Dr David Nias. He says modern life in general imposes stresses that were largely unknown until recently, as people are given more freedom and thus forced to make more choices. And no one has as much liberty, as few guidelines and as many choices as a Princess of Wales set free from the bonds of royal propriety. He talks about 'the situation specific model'.

'You adapt your behaviour according to the role you've been given in life,' he says. 'So if you get a job as a salesman, you fit in to what you see as the perception of the role. So she must be very aware of the role she's been given, so she's trying to model herself to make the most of that to the best of her ability, which is a situation not many people are in.

'Roles for most people, at least in the old days, were very straightforward. Grew up, went to work in the coalmine, got married, had children; it was all clear cut. Whereas what's really changed in recent times is that people have much more freedom, which in a way makes life very much more difficult because we have to make choices. We're more responsible for what we do. That, of course, increases both the scope for improving one's life and for making mistakes.' With hindsight, the visit to be televised watching a child's heart operation was an example of the latter, says Dr Nias.

'She needs more back-up and support, because someone experienced would have predicted that sort of reaction so they could have at least tucked her hair away,' he says. 'One wonders why, when the other nurses and theatre staff were under instructions, she was an exception. It would be embarrassing for the theatre manager to tell her, which is why she should have her own managers and experts advising her, which would make her job less stressful. To take on the whole responsibility herself is asking too much. Diana's been thrown in at the deep end and is trying to adapt to her position, and, being under stress, it's very difficult because things tend to snowball, get worse and worse. She just can't relax.'

But no amount of wise PR counsel will have any effect unless Diana can be persuaded to act on it, and, in that respect, Dr Sidney Crown reckons she is her own worst enemy. 'I feel she must be going against the advice of friends and advisors,' he says. 'Her own self-will, her own narcissism, pushes her on to repeat these things over and over again. I do find it all astonishing. It's all part of her exhibitionistic personality, the self-centred part of her, the need to attach enormous importance to her body. It all suggests a lack of what is psychologically called insight – seeing herself as other people see her. I think what she picks up in some strange way is that there will be a significant proportion of people who won't see it in the same way as many sophisticated people.

'The less sophisticated see it rather straightforwardly: "Isn't it fantastic, she kisses people with AIDS, she might catch something," they say. "Isn't it fantastic that she goes and talks to kids in the children's home." "Isn't it amazing that she goes into an operating theatre and doesn't faint." There are millions of people who watch television all over the country who are not sophisticated socially or psychologically and don't see things in a complicated way and would see everything she does as being very positive. They would see all her detractors as people who are pressurizing her and trying to wreck her life.'

Dr Crown believes Diana has become something of a loose cannon, unwilling to listen to the advice of those with her best interests at heart. 'It sounds as if there's some problem going on with her therapists,' he says. 'I don't think any therapist, either conventional or alternative or fringe, would advise her to go and watch those operations.

'If you're dealing with someone as difficult as Di, first of all, you'd talk about it for some time. When you realized you were up against it because she was determined to do it, you'd say, "You realize I don't think this is a good idea, I don't think it fits into what we've been doing together. On the other hand, if you're absolutely determined to do it, that's the way it has go to be. You in the end have got to make the decision." You can't live people's lives for them, and you can't act as thought police so, in the end, it would be a case of talking it through as a therapist, and then she would do what she wants to do.

'She's never really had an opportunity or the mental where-withal to develop the sort of independent personality that most people develop very early on during childhood. In adolescence, then in early childhood, you establish what is technically known as identity, that is, how we understand ourselves and how we differentiate ourselves from other people. Many problems presented to psychotherapists are from people either who have fractured identities or who have never properly established one. Often they'll say, "I don't really know who I am, and I've come here to try to find out." In a sense, Diana has really had problems with establishing her identity, and she tends to diffuse it into all sorts of areas.'

One of these is the operating theatre. For Diana, standing in on an operation gives her the opportunity to identify with the heroic achievements of a theatre team who can truly say of the patients, 'their lives in our hands'.

'She probably got herself hypnotized by the whole business,' says Dr Crown. 'Illness, death, surgery, people who dress up in green outfits which are not meant to be stylish but look stylish. It's very much her thing. She dresses in designer track suits and designer trainers, but she's like a surgeon really, in the sense that she's a histrionic figure who likes to be photographed, just as surgeons like to be seen in their clothes. Both sorts of outfits are fashionable and trendy and also, in a strange sort of way, sexually attractive. Designer tracksuits are, and nurses dressed for theatre, who have virtually nothing on except those gowns, are very sexually attractive.'

Despite all these problems Diana's charismatic approach set new standards in royal visits. Her combination of beauty, glamour and sensitivity proved an intoxicating cocktail compared with the low-key approach adopted by other royals. As the level of adulation grew, so she began to believe her own publicity.

'She's got it into her head that she has special powers now because who doesn't love a hug or a kiss from someone special?' says Mary Spillane. 'We all do. We'd like it from anyone, let alone a princess. But she's naïve enough to think that she has more power, or that she's better at it than the average person or the rest of the Royal Family. Because the rest of the Royal Family aren't so engaging physically she feels that she's superior to them, and that she's what the country wants.' As time went on Diana began to feel she had a sort of divine right to be at the centre of any national tragedy. Unfortunately for her, the Palace saw things differently.

TWELVE

LIVING DOLL

'She'll be able to carry on this song and dance for another 15 or 20 years.'

MARY SPILLANE, IMAGE CONSULTANT

J ust when Diana thought things could not get any worse, something happened that struck at the very core of her being. It had been all she could do to hold things together after the bad publicity surrounding her remarks to Tiggy Legge-Bourke and the furore over her relationship with Will Carling, but the episode that affected her more deeply than either of these was the revelation that she had cellulite, a condition that produces an unsightly 'orange-peel' appearance on the surface of the skin and afflicts eight out of ten women.

No one knew better than Diana the importance of her physical perfection to the myth of the fairytale princess. Like many women in their mid-thirties, she will probably examine herself from time to time for signs of the tell-tale wrinkles that could spell the beginning of the end of her image of untarnished youth and beauty, perhaps looking in the mirror to detect any trace of crows' feet around the eyes. But the first evidence of her own mortality was spotted not above the shoulders but below the waist. A sharp-eyed photographer, equipped with a telescopic lens, provided the world with evidence of the awful truth: Diana had lumpy legs.

The effect this had on the Princess was there for all to see the very next day when she made her regular trip to the Harbour Club. On a bright spring morning, which was the warmest of that year so far, instead of wearing the regulation sweatshirt, which left her legs open to public view, she wore an ankle-length cashmere overcoat. The coat covered the damaging evidence that no amount of working out had succeeded in alleviating.

Aware of the Long Tom lenses focused on her from the club's perimeter walls, Diana played out a bizarre ritual as she left by the back door. In an extraordinary bid to hide her face, she wore dark glasses and descended the short flight of steps in a crablike manner, her face to the wall and one hand pressed to the brickwork for balance. When she reached the foot of the steps, she persisted in the charade by walking towards her car with her head at right angles to her direction of travel, before climbing into the driver's seat, having achieved her aim of protecting her face but at great cost to her dignity.

The next day's papers were full of it, and, aware that the cellulite story was spiralling out of control, a friend of Diana's told the press that the marks seen in photographer Glenn Harvey's pictures had been caused by sitting on the leather seats of her BMW. But Harvey pointed out that when he took his photographs she had not been in the car for more than an hour, as she was returning to it rather than coming from it. Another version attributed the marks to the Harbour Club's bar stools. These inconsistencies only fuelled the debate, and, in a final desperate bid to rebut the story, Diana authorized her personal fitness trainer Jenni Rivett to make it clear the claims were 'hurtful, demeaning and unfounded'.

'There have been thousands of pictures taken of the Princess arriving at and leaving gyms, and this is the only bad one,' added Rivett. 'I think they've tampered with it. Either that, or the photographs were shot in such appallingly bad light that it would have distorted anyone's body, no matter how good it was.' The arguments failed to convince, however, and the consequences are serious for a woman who sets such store by her appearance.

'This [the cellulite issue] is enough to send her underground for at least six months,' says image consultant Mary Spillane. 'The charge of cellulite in your mid-thirties is just enough to send you to your grave, really. A year ago Demi Moore was caught by some nasty paparazzi in just the same way in Miami with her kids just prior to filming *Striptease*. She retreated to get herself in shape.

'Diana's high and mighty attitude in the last two years about being the victim and also being Miss Perfect, the body beautiful and quite the role model, has actually built up a great deal of resentment in certain sections of the press – particularly with women journalists – which is backfiring on her. It's almost like, "Gotcha! You're no better than we are."

'It also lends credence to the notion that she's a bit of a poseur exerciser, in as much as, if she's been working out this vigorously, there should be an element of aerobic work going on, which leaves you looking ghastly. You work up a sweat, the face swells, you turn red, your hair gets stuck to your head. You'd never leave the gym looking like she does. She leaves looking quite perfect, like she's just done weights and things like that. It shows that she's probably still dieting quite rigorously and pumping iron but not really doing the kind of work-out that would give you the sort of fitness that she's looking for and also get rid of all that garbage, like cellulite, that sets in in your thirties.

'I fear that this is setback material, and I really hope that she can rise above it, which is why I'm saying it's so self-defeating going from one body obsession to another. She's got to move on to the cerebral level if she's going to pull herself out of things. You know, studying or reading or something like that.'

Diana must have anticipated with some apprehension the day that news would break of the first flaw in her bodily perfection. For years she had done everything she could to stave off the ravages of time. In her early thirties, the Princess was reported to have travelled to a clinic in Spain, following the birth of her sons, for revolutionary therapy designed to stave off the onset of the ugly blemishes by improving skin tone and curing muscle ache.

Quite why a woman who maintains a diet of lean meat, salads (without dressing) and mineral water in pursuit of the body beautiful should have fallen prey to such a condition is something of a mystery. She even followed the experts' other tip: to exercise regularly.

But Diana's healthy regime was not all that it seemed. For the angst-ridden Princess is well known for having a soft spot for chocolates, and it is telling that when her favourite son wanted to comfort her in the wake of the unseemly revelations concerning her affair with James Hewitt she says the gift he chose was a box of chocolates. Opinions are divided on what actually causes cellulite, but one school of thought attributes it to an accumulation of toxins caused by a high intake of tea, coffee, alcohol or processed foods, like Diana's favourite confections.

Other experts claim that cellulite is simply a build-up of fat just beneath the skin surface and is best combated with a disciplined programme of exercise. On the face of it Diana is diligent in this area. Her visits to the gym are the one constant in her varied daily schedule. But it is what she does when she is there that is vital to her well-being. We have described in chapter three the key social role her visits play in her life, and some observers are beginning to wonder whether working out comes a poor second to making friends. Others speculate that she may be concentrating on the wrong sort of toning up. Photographs of her in strapless gowns reveal an impressive pair of shoulders and well-toned arm muscles, and it was Sophie Rhys-Jones who, during her courtship with Prince Edward, reportedly said: 'She is beginning to look like a Gladiator.' But the press-ups and weight training that have produced such a powerful upper body do nothing for her lower limbs.

Of one thing we can be sure: Diana's tendency to explore every possible means of turning back the clock. She is already having the sort of acupuncture sessions that might help by improving her circulation, but an enticing array of alternative therapies remain untried. These range from the esoterically named Thalgo Detoxifying Frigithalgo – a process that involves smearing the lower body with a seaweed-smelling, brown gel – to the more straight-forward Universal Contour Wrap, which involves wrapping the body in a detoxifying clay solution that shrinks as it dries. The most drastic measure she could resort to is liposuction, a surgical means of removing the offending fat. Image consultant Mary Spillane reckons Diana will turn to plastic surgery more and more as the years pass. No one knows better than the Princess that time is the greatest enemy.

With a potentially catastrophic drop in her official status

following her divorce, maintaining her looks will be an essential part of holding on to her position as the public's darling. So are her days at the top numbered? Agony aunt Claire Rayner certainly thinks her popularity is set to wane. 'Watch it mate, she is cracking in all directions,' she warns the authors. 'It is very, very temporary. It is not the deep abiding sort. She thinks it's going to last for ever, it's not. The public all over the world is very fickle. Give it another few years, and they're going to start photographing the incipient dewlaps [the flesh at the throat that becomes flaccid with age]. What will happen to her is the same as what happens to all these icons who just marry into fame. I can't be doing with non-doers personally. This is strictly a personal reaction, but, as a good feminist, these women who achieve their fame simply because of who they marry depress me deeply.'

Mary Spillane does not share Rayner's pessimism at the length of Diana's shelf-life, however. 'She probably has another 15 years as an image icon, because of all the things that women have at their disposal today,' she says, 'and from then on there is the surgeon's knife, which is subtle and available. Take Fergie, for example. She could immediately look ten years younger if she saw a plastic surgeon because her face has totally dropped at a very young age. There are things you can do to your eyes, little nips and tucks, without the full-blown face lift that most people are familiar with.

'The American culture is to start to do it younger. You have little things done, and no one ever knows. I don't reckon Diana has had anything done, there's no need yet. She's not too young for it, she just doesn't need it because she's so fit. Fergie, on the other hand, could use an eye lift and have her jowls seen to, too. But even she could get away with it by saying she'd been on holiday, or on a diet, or just got fitter.

'Diana, with everything that is available today and because of her past, will be able to carry on this song and dance for another 15 or 20 years. There's life in the old girl yet. Look at the film stars in America who are still catwalk models or making fitness videos, people like Raquel Welch, Jane Fonda and so on. They all use this stuff.'

The comparison is particularly apt, for no royal has ever traded on their beauty as successfully as Diana. Never was this more evident than when she dazzled the cream of American society at a glittering charity event in December 1995. The VIPs crowded into the sumptuous ballroom of the New York Hilton were entranced. They had expected a 'real-life' princess, but what they got was a Hollywood-style beauty. The daringly low-slung Jacques Azagury evening gown drew all eyes to her cleavage, and even Henry Kissinger could not resist a surreptitious glance as he greeted her with a peck on the cheek.

Diana was there to receive the Outstanding Achievement Award at the United Cerebral Palsy charity dinner, her reward not for years of arduous fieldwork but for meeting and greeting people, on occasions such as this one, more than 3000 miles from home. It was her unchallenged position as the world's number one superstar that had enabled the organizers to charge 900 of the great, the good and the simply loaded to part with £800 apiece merely to dine in her presence. No one knew better than Diana that it was not enough for her just to be a princess, she had to look like a royal straight out of Central Casting.

Mary Spillane says the dress so much admired by Kissinger and every other man in the room 'defied foundation'. Spillane has followed Diana's transition from frumpy Sloane teenager to global fashion icon with a professional eye. 'Her clothes are getting more and more revealing, and they border on the undignified,' she says. 'She walks a very fine line. On occasions she can't be wearing a bra, for example, or, because of the way things are cut, she obviously isn't wearing any knickers. She'll be wearing a G-string.

'OK, women know this, and while men don't know what's going on they just think, Oh, crikey, that's low cut, or whatever. I think she's very proud of her body and herself.'

Dr Sidney Crown agrees: 'She now wears dresses that are very revealing. Initially her clothes showed her sexual inexperience, then her sexual frustration and now they show her sexual bravado.'

Her sexy self-image even has some role in her relationship with her sons. At the age of 13 William was a bundle of hormones, and his bedroom walls at Eton and Kensington Palace reflected his new-found interest in the opposite sex. Pictures of American supermodel Cindy Crawford featured most prominently, and, when she arrived in London to promote the relaunch of Pepsi-Cola in the spring of 1996, Diana invited her to the Kensington Palace to meet her boys over lunch. Far from being a straightforward if rather peculiar treat for the young Princes, the visit was, in fact, an opportunity for Diana to reassert her primacy as the most glamorous figure in their lives. She gave the game away by later telling friends: 'She's shorter than you think.' (At 5ft 9in, the cover girl was almost two inches shorter than her royal hostess.)

We can only speculate on how the meeting went, but Crawford cannot fail to have been intimidated at meeting the most famous woman in the world on home ground. By allowing William to meet his fantasy woman in the flesh, Diana effectively demystified her. His own mother was not only taller but more beautiful. When Diana, dressed in a blue blazer and skirt, subsequently met Crawford in the bar of the Dorchester Hotel in Park Lane it is unlikely she relayed the information that William had later confessed to being bored at the lunch and had removed pictures of the model from his locker at Eton.

The event had echoes of an equally questionable incident a year earlier, when William and a friend argued over a centrefold of the buxom twins, Shane and Shia. The response of many mothers would have been to confiscate the offending item with a word of censure. But Diana, who was taking her sons to a rugby international in Cardiff, snatched the picture from them and neatly tore it in two, giving one blonde to her son and the other to his friend. It is almost as if she feels that by promoting this adoration of sex and glamour she will retain her own lustre in the eyes of her children. Her self-esteem is so low she cannot conceive of them loving her for any other reason than the rest of the world does: her glamour. In the circumstances it is hard to see how she would have related to daughters. One royal watcher speaks for many when she says: 'How she would have treated girls doesn't even bear thinking about.'

Psychologist Susan Quilliam agrees. 'Diana is not a woman's woman, she is a man's woman, and heaven help her daughters if she had any. Thank goodness she had sons. It's really, really clear that she gets on beautifully with her sons, but I do not believe that if she had had daughters there would have been such a strong bond.'

Diana is not only aware of her sex appeal but also actively exploits it. The plunging neckline that confronted Henry Kissinger and his friends displayed only one aspect of her bodily charms. As Dr Sidney Crown points out, it is not the only part of her anatomy she uses to attract attention. He cites her habit of showing off her legs for waiting cameramen each time she gets out of a car.

It is an image she is working hard to preserve. 'I think she wants to put the best face on herself,' concludes Dr Dennis Friedman. 'That's why she goes to the gym. She wants to keep looking good. That's why she dresses in this expensive way. I suppose she doesn't want anyone to see her not looking at her best. She'd go to any lengths to keep herself looking good, because she can't imagine anybody would be concerned for her otherwise. She has to have something that would make them care, and she sees that as her appearance and being a good person.'

Dr David Nias reckons part of her motivation is to give the public what it wants. 'I think she's aware that she mustn't let people down,' he says, 'the people who do love her. So she's got to be at her best. She may not be seeking adulation for herself but for the general public who idolize her. There's a sort of fascination with the Royal Family. She's someone who people can identify with. Her story's like a fairytale, and her position is rather like that of the sports star who's got fans whom he mustn't let down. So he might boast far more than he would normally, for example, to live up to the fans' expectations.'

Diana's image today is a far cry from the day of her engagement in 1981 when, as a hunch-shouldered teenager, she posed for pictures in the garden of Buckingham Palace. Observant royal watchers noticed a tell-tale crease betraying where the hem on the skirt of her smart Harrods suit had been hastily lowered for the occasion. It was an early illustration of the strict dress code imposed upon entrants to the royal circle by the Palace old guard.

But even then there were signs that the bride-to-be was not the demure young thing she appeared. An episode that occurred in the grounds of the kindergarten where she worked when news of her relationship with Charles broke can now be seen in a new light. With a decorative tot tucker under each arm, Diana had posed for photographers, declaring, 'You know I cannot say anything about the Prince or my feelings for him.' Her choice of dress, however, had a lot to say about Diana. Her skirt was diaphanous in the autumn sunlight and showed her legs in glorious silhouette.

It has since become clear that, far from considering this a trick of the light, Charles saw it as her first foray into media manipulation. A friend who was having breakfast with him when the next day's papers arrived says he was furious. He immediately telephoned Diana, in the friend's hearing, and demanded to know why she had done it. When he got off the phone he said she had replied: 'I thought they [the press] would go away if I did a picture for them.' This can now be seen as the moment that Diana hit upon a winning combination of sex appeal and maternal devotion.

Nevertheless Diana still had a lot to learn. 'In the early days she was catapulted into the limelight, quite unprepared,' says Mary Spillane. 'It was not really a media age then, the royals were not on the front pages all the time. She used one of the Sloaney dressmakers, Bill Pashley from Battersea. I know him quite well, he's a lovely chap, but his stuff was very safe, country Sloaney gear, which she used to wear until everything started to be remarked upon. The experts said she needed help matching the bows on her shoes to the bows on her hat.'

When Diana declared early on in her marriage: 'Clothes are for the job, they've got to be practical,' she knew few would believe her, so she added: 'Sometimes I can be a little outrageous, which is quite nice, but only sometimes.' One such occasion occurred when she turned out for her first official engagement with Princess Grace of Monaco at the Goldsmith's Hall in the City of London. Her choice of a strapless, taffeta ball gown was criticized by senior members of the establishment for showing too much cleavage, but Diana knew she had awakened interest in a glamour-hungry public.

'She started to enjoy the limelight,' says Spillane. 'She grew into the limelight, and it was the adoration that she never got from the family she was starting to get from the public, and she loved it. That's why she kept giving them more of what they loved.

'Anna Harvey from *Vogue* was a great influence on her. She would send clothes over to her with little notes advising her to simplify things, not to wear so many contrived outfits, because when Sloane women dressed up they really got dressed up. It was not terribly international, it was too fitted and fussy and detailed and twitty for the modern age. It really looked quite silly with all the bows and the tweeness. And because she was a tall gangly girl it looked even more contrived on her. It would have been fine on someone petite, but on a taller and more striking woman Sloane style looked silly, frankly. So *Vogue* was a great influence on her and helped her to get it together. Then she started to enjoy clothes and fashion, and she liked the fact that the press and the people reacted the way they did to her.'

She turned to the hottest names in international haute couture. Catherine Walker, Bruce Oldfield, Victor Edelstein and Bellville Sassoon all rallied to the cause. Her love for fashion became so all-consuming that it even caused a rift with the Palace. Black is a fashion staple, but protocol dictates that royals do not wear it unless they are in mourning. Diana considered this something approaching an infringement of her liberties, and since her separation from Charles she has regularly flouted the rule. In time she became so well known for her dazzling range of designer outfits that she was forced to adopt the business suit in a bid to be taken seriously as a working woman rather than a mere fashion plate.

Alongside this transformation of her wardrobe ran an intensive and expensive grooming operation. Kevin Shanley at Headlines in South Kensington persuaded her to add highlights to her mousy hair, returning it to the blonde shade of her childhood years. From that moment she seemed to grow in confidence, and the hunch-shouldered posture disappeared for ever. As her preoccupation with her appearance intensified, she graduated to two of London's top stylists, Sam McKnight, who cut her hair every six weeks, and Daniel Galvin, who touched up her highlights at his Mayfair salon. She now spends £3600 a year on hair colouring alone.

The make-over didn't end there. Manicurists, beauticians and pedicurists were summoned to Kensington Palace to work their magic at an annual cost of £2600, while another £1600 was spent on body-care products; £500 on skin-care products; £300 on make-up; £800 on sun creams; and £240 on multivitamins. As Earl Spencer once shrewdly observed of his youngest daughter: 'Diana doesn't understand about money, she's no experience of it.'

The immaculately turned out Princess then required equally immaculate accessories. Mindful of the adage, you are what you drive, Diana risked royal disapproval in 1992 by ignoring the staid saloons offered by British manufacturers in favour of a sleek, German-made Mercedes convertible. The resulting controversy forced her to send it back, but it was not long before her turbo-charged ego won the day. She duly invested in a second foreign-made convertible, this time a sporty Audi. The importance of having a car to match her image was demonstrated early in 1996 when she took delivery of a state-of-the-art 5-series BMW, valued at £40,000 but at no cost to her. The makers were more than compen-sated by a royal endorsement during an impromptu press conference on the pavement outside the Marylebone clinic of her osteopath Michael Skipwith. 'Isn't it lovely,' she said. 'I'm only borrowing it, but it's great.'

This carefully assembled ensemble set flash bulbs popping around the globe. And just as publishers discovered that her face on the cover increased sales of newspapers and magazines all over the world, Diana began to realize the full extent of her media pulling power. She put that power to the ultimate test in 1991 when she telephoned the French photographer Patrick Demarchelier at his apartment in New York and gave him the most prestigious commission of his illustrious career: the chance to photograph her for the cover of *Vogue*. Her hubris had never been more vividly illustrated, for no one at *Vogue*, least of all its editor Liz Tilberis, knew anything of her plans.

Nor were they the only ones to be kept in the dark. According to her then press secretary, Geoffrey Crawford, this was Diana at her devious best. No one at Kensington Palace knew about the call or the subsequent photo session at a London studio. Over lunch with Tilberis, Diana provided her with the pictures she liked best from the Demarchelier shoot. In a move that might have helped to silence her critics, Diana insisted on a reciprocal plug for the Royal Ballet, one of her pet causes. But no one was fooled by the window dressing, and the cover caused a sensation around the world, just as she had anticipated.

Still a woman under 30 at the time of the shoot, Diana needed little help from sympathetic lighting or delicate airbrushing to come across as a vision of youthful beauty. And she is not about to let it fade without a fight. According to Mary Spillane, it's the aspect of her life at which she works hardest.

'She has a lot of time on her hands,' says Spillane. 'She talks about all this work that she does, but it would be lovely to have a life like that. She might have to open something, or go along to a dinner or a luncheon, but the rest of the time is spent sorting out her wardrobe, or going to the gym. The children are away at school so she doesn't really have anything else to do. She's not studying anything. She's not learning anything new. She's getting therapy. Everything is me-centred.

'And as for this notion that she's conquered bulimia, that obsession has just been replaced by a fitness mania. She's very self-obsessed. It's a modern phenomenon. There are a lot of women like her. A lot of working women, for example, who don't have family and other commitments, who might be doing a job but who spend the rest of the time maintaining their body. They create this vision of perfection, but no one dares approach it because it's such perfection. I think for any guy to approach Diana would take great courage.'

This glamorization process is the last thing the Princess needs, according to Claire Rayner. 'What worries me about her is that, with the aid of the media, she is being made into some glamorous icon when she's the last person who ought to be an icon,' she says. 'All her achievements rest on three penises: she married one and produced two more. She's done nothing else. And to idolize the woman for that reason, and that reason alone, is ridiculous. Pop stars at least sell a record or two. Film stars at least get up early in the morning and do a day's work. But what has *she* actually done?'

THIRTEEN

UPSTAIRS, DOWNSTAIRS

'You either resign or go to work in the gardens.'

THE PRINCESS OF WALES

Nowhere is Diana's growing instability more evident than in her dealings with servants. While she can slip into the persona that has made her the most-loved royal in history for her public engagements, it is behind closed palace doors that Diana emerges in different colours. There, the charming princess metamorphoses into a difficult employer. Confidentiality clauses written in to each staff member's contract of employment do something to stem the flow of stories emanating from Kensington Palace, but tales abound, nevertheless, of insulting behaviour, smashed crockery and shouting. Those who do talk – and it is always off the record – stress that no one is immune to her mood swings: everyone from her most senior aide to the lowliest chambermaid has experienced her wrath.

Soon after her uncalled-for remarks to the royal nanny Tiggy Legge-Bourke Diana lost one of her most trusted lieutenants, her private secretary Patrick Jephson. He had remained loyal to her when she separated from Charles and even stayed at his post after the *Panorama* interview, which sparked the resignation of her press secretary Geoffrey Crawford. But, one day, she went too far even for the phlegmatic Jephson. So 'outrageous and dreadful' was the personal insult she directed at him that, within hours, he had handed in his notice, cleared out the desk in his office at St James's Palace and set off to Devon to lick his wounds at home. The seriousness of the rift was such that it was obviously impossible for the two to work together a moment longer.

Less than 24 hours after Jephson's abrupt departure, the Princess lost her personal assistant Nicky Cockell. She had accompanied Diana on a politically sensitive visit to Argentina only two months earlier and was the lynchpin in the organization of her official engagements and foreign trips. The vivacious blonde aide was also one of the most popular members of staff at St James's Palace.

The same day saw the departure of the driver Steve Davies, who had also suffered from Diana's outbursts. So unhappy was he that he once said he would rather be a long-distance lorry driver than chauffeur to the most glamorous woman in the world. According to Palace sources, Diana had not exchanged a civil word with Davies since he angered her the previous year by befriending Will Carling and driving him to speaking engagements on a freelance basis. When she heard that the two men had been playing golf together, Diana reprimanded him with: 'He's my friend not yours.'

Psychiatrist Dr Sidney Crown reckons Diana would not be so concerned with her chauffeur and her friend exchanging confidences. 'I think she'd be less worried about the things he and Carling gossiped about and more concerned that she sees the chauffeur as her property,' says Dr Crown. 'What's more, if Will Carling took him away, she would see that as a rivalrous thing.'

If Davies thought that the end of his royal duties meant his days of royal displeasure were over he was badly mistaken. Separated from his wife Sue, the mother of his young daughter, the handsome Davies had begun a relationship with Diana's dresser Helen Walsh. A few weeks after his services were dispensed with, Davies was caught in a late-night tryst with Walsh, at 28, four years his junior. The Princess, returning from one of her lonely late-night drives, spotted his car outside her dresser's flat overlooking the courtyard at Kensington Palace.

Furiously, she began hammering on Walsh's front door, shouting at the top of her voice for the pair to 'come out at once'.

The startled lovers scrambled into their clothes and arrived at the door looking shocked and dishevelled. They were greeted by a Princess described by one witness as 'a woman possessed' and were forced to endure in silence a long and blistering tirade. It ended with Davies being escorted from the Palace precincts.

Dr Crown interprets the incident as yet another manifestation of Diana's all-consuming need to dominate others. 'She has to have complete control of people she's involved with, and that is one of the reasons why relationships break down, because nobody can tolerate being controlled,' says Dr Crown. 'Friendship is an egalitarian thing.'

'When he [Davies] got into the act by forming a relationship with the dresser, Diana would have been incapable of dealing with that. She would feel that somehow she was being pushed out of a relationship that really was hers: hers with the dresser, hers with the chauffeur, hers with Carling. Those are the things that belong to her, and she can't tolerate the sort of interaction, which most people would consider part of normal life. She is so self-centred that she has to have complete control of all these people.

'The business of people losing control is so common among famous people. They say it about a lot of politicians. They'll give a television interview and be all sweetness and light, and then curse and swear immediately afterwards. When something triggers off the sort of person who hasn't got a really well-integrated personality, they go completely over the top, shouting and screaming.' Despite her serene exterior Dr Crown sees Diana as someone who could 'really lose control'. This phrase is a chilling echo of one of the main findings of the Palace-sponsored psychiatric report described in chapter one.

What secretary Jephson and chauffeur Davies witnessed, Prince Charles had experienced in the earliest days of their marriage. What the public have seen of Diana is what the Prince saw right up to their wedding day. One of his closest confidants told the authors: 'She was sweetness and light until they got married. She would go and sit with him on the riverbank while he fished and stand in the butts with him while he was shooting. Never uttering a cross or critical word. But the moment she was his wife, all that changed. It wasn't until then he had the slightest inkling of her violent temper.'

They had only recently returned from their honeymoon and were holidaying with the rest of the Royal Family at Balmoral when Charles experienced for the first time the full ferocity of her rage. 'Many things in the room had been smashed,' said one guest. 'Bedside tables had been knocked over and lamps broken. His Royal Highness had obviously retreated to the dressing room during the night and slept there.'

This contrast between her public poise and her private instability was also evident when Diana returned from a barn-storming performance at a charity fund-raiser only to rant at staff at the Palace.

'It fits in this paradoxical way with someone who has great difficulty with impulse control,' says Dr Crown. 'One of the most amazing things in some people who are public figures is the way they can behave in such an uncontrolled way in their private lives, and yet they appear to be models of formality and control in every other bit of their lives.'

Dr Dorothy Rowe, on the other hand, claims such behaviour is understandable in a young woman under the pressure Diana finds herself. 'We all shout and scream to relieve our tensions in a situation where we know we can get away with it,' she says. 'Society is full of people who behave extremely well when they are in the company of strangers but, once they get home, let rip. She's behaving in a way that many people behave in when they get very tense, very angry but have to represent themselves as very very calm. What you then do is to express it as soon as you can. I often walk in through my front door and resort to the kind of language that I'd learned back in Australia, and which I wouldn't dream of using in public here, but I haven't got a house full of servants listening to me scream and yell.'

It was just such screaming and yelling that made life unbearable for a long line of people who had to work alongside the Princess. The history of her poor relations with staff dates back to the early eighties, when the publicly demure Diana was soon dubbed 'the mouse that roared' as she exerted her new-found authority over the royal household. First to go was Charles's devoted valet, Stephen Barry, who had joined the staff of Buckingham Palace 16 years earlier as a humble footman. Before the royal wedding he had made the mistake of barring her from her fiancé's study. Soon after this episode he paid the price, leaving Charles's service describing his master's wife as a 'spoilt brat'.

His departure proved the first of many. At one stage the scale of the exodus was of embarrassing proportions, and Diana's brother, Charles, was forced to come to her aid, declaring: 'She is an exceptionally kind and thoughtful person, but nobody is saying she's a fool.'

More recently the spate of desertions has not let up. In November 1993 her chauffeur Simon Solari defected to Prince Charles, ostensibly because he had too little to do. Her equerry, Captain Edward Musto, left five months later to return to the Marines. Cook Mervyn Wycherley departed after 23 years' service in 1995; the same year butler Harold Brown was made redundant. Brown's replacement, his assistant Paul Burrell, is now referred to as 'the only man Diana really trusts'. It is just the sort of testimonial the son of a Coal Board lorry driver could do without. Its equivalent in footballing parlance is the club chairman's promise: 'The manager has my full confidence and support.' The unfortunate supremo is invariably sacked within days.

One woman who has experienced the unnerving extremes of Diana's character is Marion Cox, the Highgrove-based groom who helped James Hewitt teach William and Harry to ride. The boys doted on her, giving her the nickname Mrs Flopsy, but when they began visiting her home to see the rabbit and guinea pig she kept there, Diana turned against her. She gave her a stark choice: 'You either resign or go to work in the gardens.' When Cox heard of Diana's jealous reaction to Tiggy Legge-Bourke's relationship with her charges, she said: 'I think that's why I got the push.'

The reason we know so much about the goings-on in Diana's inner sanctums is very much a sign of the times. Today's newspaper editors are keenly aware of the intense public interest in scoops about the House of Windsor and are prepared to pay handsome sums for tales from the royal sculleries. Brought up to be a lady of the house at a time when servants could be relied upon to be discreet and deferential, Diana was traumatized to discover that stories about her private life were being sold by those who became privy to them in the course of their duties. Having gone out of her way to befriend Oliver Hoare's chauffeur Barry Hodge, she had every reason to believe that her courtesy would be rewarded with discretion. What a shock, therefore, to discover that in return for £30,000 of Rupert Murdoch's money he had revealed details of her relationship with the art dealer to the *News of the World*.

'Servants have always gossiped,' says Dr Rowe, 'it's just that now they get money for their gossip.' However, she thinks Diana could be an example of someone who believes that what is sauce for the royal goose is certainly not sauce for the proletarian gander. 'Today people are aware of politicians telling us noble things, while, at the same time, doing all sorts of scurrilous things,' she says. 'Mrs Thatcher was on television the other day talking about the wickedness of weapons, while her son was busy selling them.' She recognizes, however, that in the outmoded class structure in which Diana's upbringing was conducted, the personal lives of staff were of no account to their masters: 'Servants weren't ever supposed to have relationships, were they? They'd be dismissed if they were discovered even having a little romance.'

In such a stilted domestic climate the romance between Diana's chauffeur and her dresser would be likely to cause their mistress 'hurt and envy', says Dr Rowe. On the other hand there could, she says, have been an entirely different reason for the Princess's outburst: 'Suppose she'd just ignored it. Suppose she'd driven in, seen the car there and just quietly taken herself off to bed and then a story was leaked to the papers suggesting Diana allows this licentious behaviour in her household. That wouldn't have looked good, would it? People would have said it was not a proper place for a future heir to the throne to be brought up.'

Dr Friedman sees quite a different reason for Diana's outrage at her servants' indiscretion: 'They're all scapegoats,' he says, 'they're dependent. I suppose what she sees in them is the helpless part of herself because she's also trapped. As a child she was very conscious of her dependent needs, and they had not been satisfied. When things go wrong for her in this grown-up world, she is angry with the dependent part of herself. When she's angry with herself, she gets depressed. It's easy to be angry with other dependent people. It's a form of role reversal. She can unload those feelings on to other people.'

For those who manage to stay on the right side of Diana, there are bonuses aplenty. One who knows all about the plus-side of royal duties is Victoria Mendham, one of three secretaries who work in the Princess's private office. When Diana decided to take a Caribbean holiday and realized she didn't have a friend available to go with her, she invited Mendham. The secretary accompanied the Princess on the island of Barbuda at the sumptuous K Club, where her room for the week would have cost her more than three months' salary. The somewhat incongruous pair swam, exercised and dined together. It must have been the holiday of a lifetime for young Mendham. And it is to be hoped that she savoured it while she could. There is one virtual certainty in life on Diana's payroll: that you will soon be off it.

FOURTEEN

HEWITT: UNFINISHED BUSINESS

'James was utterly fanatical about the way he looked.'

EMMA STEWARDSON, FORMER GIRLFRIEND OF CAPTAIN HEWITT

J ames Hewitt was Diana's Action Man in almost every sense. He was a soldier, and he was a doll. As the dashing cavalry officer he fulfilled many of her romantic imaginings. Out of uniform, however, she could dress him any way she wished. And she did. She invested thousands of pounds on him. Out went the department-store blazers and cotton-mix shirts; in came bespoke suits and silk ties. As she told James Gilbey on the infamous Squidgygate tape:

DIANA: 'James Hewitt. Entirely dressed him from head to foot, that man. Cost me quite a bit.'

GILBEY: 'I bet he did. At your expense?'

DIANA: 'Yeah.'

GILBEY: 'What, he didn't even pay you to do it?'

DIANA: 'No.'

GILBEY: 'God, that's extravagant, darling.'

DIANA: 'Well, I am, aren't I? Anything that will make people happy.'

GILBEY: 'No, you mustn't do it for that, darling, because you make people happy. It's what you give them.'

Hewitt's sartorial transformation surprised many of his friends, who wondered how he could afford to dress so well on his £24,000 a year salary. Emma Stewardson, the girlfriend who stood by him for four years as she waited in vain for his affair with Diana to burn itself out, could have told them. His handmade shirts from royal shirtmaker Turnbull and Asser, his Savile Row suits and his handstitched shoes were all bought by Diana. As was the diamond-studded tie-pin and the solid gold cuff-links from the royal jewellers Asprey.

So what could have motivated Diana to show such attention to detail? 'It might be that he was a scruff, and one thing she does pay particular attention to is clothes and appearance,' says Dr Sidney Crown. 'If he was a scruff before she met him, she would have used her significant income to send him to a designer shop to get him kitted out to look the way she wanted him to look. She might even have gone along with him. Because of her powerful position as a royal compared with his as a commoner, she wanted to model him in her image. It's all a matter of control, really.'

Dr Crown believes this expensive make-over would have seriously affected the already hopelessly skewed balance of power between them. 'Most good relationships are fairly egalitarian with a great deal of give and take,' he says. 'Hewitt was, in many respects, like a toyboy though, strictly speaking, he wasn't because he was older. But he was the sort of person you can act down to. I would think that dressing him up like a model, like a puppet, would affect the relationship enormously in everyday life. It might spill over into their sex life in the sense that he might want to reassert himself: "If I'm made to feel so inferior by you dressing me up, I'll make you feel attractive by exciting you in bed." So it would have a complicated effect on the relationship, which would be mostly negative.

'He would have felt a bought man, a dressed-up man, a doll, really. After all you can dress a doll anyway you want to. The only thing that would protect him from feelings of inferiority would be his own greed. If he was a greedy guy he would take the view that material possessions are the only things that matter, and he could always sell the cuff-links once they'd split up.'

Psychologist Susan Quilliam reckons this infatuation with the outer man is all part of her unbalanced attitude to relationships. 'When she is buying a man clothes, she is saying, "Take from me everything that you want," and then, "When I've given you everything and you still don't love me enough, I'm going to take that big lump of blame, and guess where I'm going to put it? On you."

'That blaming is what happened with Charles as well. And that's what I thought when I watched them on television walking down the aisle. I went, "Oh, my God, he can't handle it, and she can't handle it." I felt as sorry for him as I did for her. She genuinely wanted to give him everything, but, unfortunately, it wasn't enough. Then, when it's not enough, who does she blame? She blames him.'

Hewitt was not the only man in her life she treated like this. For while the caddish captain may have been the only one she actually went to town on, she took a similar interest in James Gilbey's attire. The obsession is most vividly illustrated in the following exchange from the Squidgygate tape:

DIANA: 'What have you got on?'

GILBEY: 'New jeans that I bought yesterday. Green socks, a white, pink-striped shirt. . .'

DIANA: (interrupting approvingly): 'Oh, very nice.'

GILBEY: 'A dark bottle-green, V-necked jersey . . . . I'm afraid you're going to be let down by the shoes.'

DIANA: 'Go on then.'

GILBEY: 'Go on, guess.'

DIANA: (betraying an encyclopaedic knowledge of his wardrobe): 'Your brown ones?'

GILBEY: 'What?'

DIANA: 'Your brown ones . . . . No . . . no . . . those black ones.'

GILBEY: 'No, I haven't got the black ones on, darling. The black ones I would not be wearing. I only wear the black ones with my suit.'

DIANA: 'We'll get rid of those anyway.'

GILBEY: 'I have got those brown-suede ones on.'

DIANA: 'Brown-suede ones?'

GILBEY: 'Brown suede . . . Gucci.'

DIANA: 'I know . . . . I know, yes . . . I just don't like the fact it's so obvious where they came from.'

'It just shows that she's very conscious of the superficial things, of appearance, of looking your best,' says image consultant Mary Spillane. 'And the fact that she actually was seeing him at the time and was so very concerned about how he looked right down to the shoes that he was wearing just shows what kind of woman she is, and so, again, it's her actions that, in an off-the-cuff private conversation, show what she's really like. In the *Panorama* interview she shows anguish over what the press focus on, claiming that she's really involved in so many other more serious pursuits when indeed this is what she's interested in.'

The couple had met at a party in Mayfair in the late summer of 1986. He was a 28-year-old officer in the Life Guards; she was a 26-year-old princess who was unhappily married. In the finest traditions of romantic fiction, their eyes met across a crowded room. They talked, and when she told him she wanted to learn to ride again, he took the bait. He offered her lessons, and within half an hour they had arranged to meet at his Hyde Park barracks.

Their hacking took place in the early morning or evening, when they would ride in the royal park that her palace apartment overlooked. During their trots around the Serpentine the pair were accompanied by a posse of police and officials, but it was not long before she asked them to hang back or disappear. The serious flirting had begun. In the barracks after a crisp morning ride they would sit on a sofa drinking mugs of coffee, and she would pour out her frustrations with her marriage. She could not communicate with her husband and felt that she bored him. After one of their lessons she asked Hewitt to dinner at Kensington Palace.

What happened next is covered in Mills and Boon style in Anna Pasternak's *A Princess in Love*, Hewitt's story of his affair with Diana. As one of the many purple passages in the book observes: 'She knew that somewhere, lurking frightened and embarrassed, was a hungry capacity for sexuality, a need to be a fulfilled and potent woman, but it had never been encouraged.' They had a candlelit dinner for two, and, as they relaxed in her Laura Ashley-decorated sitting room, heavy with the scent of roses, it was not the red-blooded soldier who made the first move. Diana, he told Pasternak, led him by the hand to her bed.

Dr Sidney Crown has his doubts over whether everything was as Hewitt would have us believe. 'First of all you've got to realize the significance of him talking about it to another person because she's such a famous person, sexually wanted and part of the fantasies of so many people,' he says. 'For her to have taken him by the hand makes him a big man. It's not that I necessarily distrust him, but a lot of men do have a macho attitude to sex. I really wouldn't want to comment because it may not have actually happened. It seems a bit unlikely.'

Diana's needs as a woman have never been more roundly and humiliatingly exposed than in the full story of her affair with Hewitt. *A Princess in Love* spelled out the explicit details of a liaison that showed Diana as a woman with powerful sexual desires. It was she, said Hewitt, who often took the sexual initiative. Whether it was by leading him by the hand to her bedroom at Kensington Palace or by taking him to Highgrove where they slept in her bedroom close to her sons' rooms – and Althorp, where they made love by the poolside. Hewitt may have had a reputation as something of a lady's man but, if we are to believe his version of events, it was she who was the one with the insatiable appetite for love. On one occasion he spurned her advances during a picnic, and she stormed off shouting: 'How could you hurt me like this?'

'All you've got to do is to see Diana around her kids to know that she's a very sensual person,' says Susan Quilliam. 'She wouldn't be hugging them, touching them and being open with them otherwise. Then we get the picture of the emotional virgin who married Charles. She'd not yet been involved with anybody, and there is a phase that a lot of women go through when they simply like being attractive and being the centre of attention because they're attractive. Most women get that experience before they marry, and Diana didn't. In that sense she's been in limbo for the last ten years. But now she's had the time and the space to indulge her sexual power and enjoyed it.'

Susan Quilliam says the crunch question is: 'Is Diana having sex because it makes her feel more powerful, or is she having sex because it makes her feel deliciously abandoned? Is it that she's having orgasms, and it's pleasurable, and it's wonderful? There are plenty of very very sexual women who never enjoy it for themselves. They enjoy it because of the relationship it gives them with their man. I'm not saying that's what happened with Diana, because I don't know, but, from the evidence, I would suggest that the issue for her is, "Show me you love me, show me I'm important, show me. . . ." The bottom line is not, "Can I give you pleasure?" but "Do I have sexual power?" The buzz for her will be, "Great, we're doing it and you want me, and you want me and you want me." Not necessarily, "Do it to me again because I've just had my fifth orgasm," but rather, "I want to give you more because you're so important to me that I want to be important to you."'

Like Oliver Hoare, Christopher Whalley and Will Carling, Hewitt was also a victim of Diana's apparent liking for the telephone. Stewardson says: 'I used to visit James when he was stationed in Paderborn in Germany in 1990. We had a lovely time, but every day there would be a phone call from Diana at his flat. I'd be expected to hang about pretending I wasn't there. Once we were about to leave for dinner when the phone went. I stood there like a fool, all dressed up to go out. I got so fed up I shouted: "Get off the line, we're going out." He was furious with me because he said the Princess had heard me shouting, and that it was offensive. I didn't care, I was fed up to the back teeth with her. If she couldn't make a go of her marriage, why the hell couldn't she find her own man and leave mine alone.'

Diana, however, was not yet ready to end her relationship with Hewitt. In him she had found a man whose preoccupations in many departments closely matched her own. There is a telling passage in Pasternak's book describing the Princess's obsession with her physique. 'She spent hours lying in bed at night dissecting her body endlessly, enumerating it's deficiencies, telling herself that she was not good enough, that she was lacking,' wrote Pasternak.

Hewitt shared this fixation with appearance. 'James was utterly fanatical about the way he looked. It was an obsession that quite worried me,' says Emma Stewardson. She even claimed that he would get pills from the vet that were designed to calm down bruises on horses. 'If he got a bruise playing polo he'd take the pills to make it go away,' she says. 'He couldn't stand anything blemishing his perfect physical appearance.' In the same way Diana employed the services of actor Terence Stamp to perfect her public speaking voice, Stewardson says Hewitt listened to recordings of Winston Churchill's wartime broadcasts to improve his.

It was this kind of detail that so offended Diana. By revealing the full extent of her hunger for physical contact, he showed her to be a woman very unlike the self-sacrificing Mother Teresa figure as whom she would have the world see her. What's more he had made money out of her, and nothing was more calculated to enrage the Princess than that. As she told *Panorama* in November 1995: 'Well, there was a lot of fantasy in that book, and it was very distressing for me that a friend of mine, who I had trusted, made money out of me. I really minded about that.' Curiously, she appeared genuinely more concerned about the financial exploitation than the disgrace that the disclosures had heaped upon her.

'To some extent Diana, apart from the *Panorama* interview, has been discreet,' says Susan Quilliam. 'She's played by the media rules, formally and informally. She hasn't kissed and told, and I think the Hewitt thing just totally took her aback, and she felt betrayed by that because it wasn't in the game plan at all.'

Princes Charles had experienced his moment of truth 16 months earlier when he had confessed his adultery with Camilla Parker Bowles to Jonathan Dimbleby. It was a revelation that had to be squeezed out of him, and, when it came, it was the most heavily disguised admission of infidelity in living memory. Asked if he had tried to be faithful to his wife, he replied: 'Yes, absolutely.' But when Dimbleby followed this up with: 'And were you?', the Prince replied: 'Yes. Until it had become irretrievably broken down – us both having tried.'

Diana gave her confession an equally slow build-up, and when she did get round to answering the question of whether she had been unfaithful, she said, 'Yes, I adored him. Yes, I was in love with him, but I was very let down.'

Diana's relationship with Hewitt came to a bitter end when he sold a sanitized version of his story to the *Daily Express* for £85,000. His interview contained no admission of the affair and no hints of any impropriety on Diana's part, but she resented him making money out of her and, thereafter, refused to take his calls. The only evidence of any further contact between them came during the *Panorama* interview, when she said Hewitt had called her to say there was nothing to worry about in Pasternak's book.

There is no doubt that theirs was a fully fledged love affair, but Diana was not about to let her heart rule her head with the press closing in. Now she is paying a high price for her involvement. Hollywood has produced a film version of their story, and Hewitt followed up his book deal with a filmed interview, in which he said that although it had never been his intention to fall in love with his royal riding pupil, it had happened. He even claimed the two of them had talked of spending the rest of their lives together.

FIFTEEN

WHAT NEXT?

'Don't think that because you've got to chapter three there aren't another 20 chapters to go.'

JEFFREY ARCHER, MULTIMILLIONAIRE NOVELIST

Denied her chance of becoming queen by the breakdown of her marriage to Prince Charles, Diana set her heart on a new job as a roving ambassador for Britain. But, as senior officials at the Palace and in the Foreign Office agitate against her plan, her chances of getting it look slim. With her beloved children at boarding school, her husband irretrievably estranged, her friendships strained by her attitude and her public role in doubt, the future looks bleak. Official anxiety over Diana's state of mind has never been more acute. Rocked by the accumulation of events, the Princess is seen as a woman on the edge. There is even concern at high levels that she could take her own life.

As the tiara begins to slip, so does her international standing. Ostracized by the Royal Family and with age creeping up on her, Diana now depends for her status solely on her role as the mother of a future king. Image consultant Mary Spillane says Diana is now in a period of transition.

'She needs to take on something new to fill her life with,' she says. 'The children are gone that's it, boarding school, goodbye. Sure she's got her charity work, which makes her very busy, but she needs something else. She needs to learn something, she needs to develop an expertise in something that's real, rather than being a Florence Nightingale figure and a clothes horse; that would fill this tremendous void that's within her.

'I am a great fan of higher education. If she threw herself into study of some sort, something that interests her, she would read, do research, develop an expertise and get out of the body and into the brain. Then she'll be less emotional and more grounded. She's interested in psychology and psycho theories of the modern world so she could extend that interest to philosophy. You don't have to be a genius to study. Sadly, Britain is very elitist about education, and she's been dismissed as a lightweight because she wasn't encouraged from a very young age. No one should be written off like that. Everyone should have access to knowledge and education and be able to carry on to whatever age they want. I think that would help her enormously.'

Dr Dorothy Rowe agrees. 'Marriage break-ups can turn out to be a wonderful opportunity to go on and achieve,' she says. 'Introvert women, like Diana, go on to do courses, get degrees, take up jobs and lead lives that they find immensely satisfying. But Diana does believe that she's not an intellectual, and she hasn't developed habits of studying and reading. Susie [Orbach] might be pointing her in the direction of literature, but if Diana developed the idea of actually getting some professional qualifications, actually learning how you help people, then that would give a great deal of point and purpose to her life.'

It would take a great effort of will on Diana's part to adopt such a disciplined approach, however. The woman who once unwisely admitted to being 'as thick as a plank' to put a child patient at ease during a visit to a hospital left school without any O levels. But, according to many in her camp, while Diana may lack formal qualifications, she has a formidable intelligence, which allows her to shine in the most high-level gatherings. Lord Archer says: 'That woman is very bright. If John Major can become prime minister on six O levels, or whatever it is, why can't Diana be accepted as a startling, impressive, shrewd and intelligent woman? There is a snobbish attitude in this country to education, that a formal certificate stating you've passed some exams shows you're clever. Try telling Joseph

Conrad that. One of the greatest writers the world has ever known. What was he? Working on tramp steamers?

'The snobby press would say, "Well, he didn't go to Oxford and read English so we really can't take him seriously." What a pompous, snobby attitude. She waltzes half those people with double firsts off the ground before they've even seen her. This is a shrewd intelligent woman who makes mistakes like all of us. I never underestimate her. I never sit in front of her and think, Well, I'm so much cleverer than you, this will just be a dawdle, I'm on my toes all the time. I sit on the edge of my seat, waiting to hear what her next sentence will be, just like I used to with Margaret [Thatcher].

'She has charisma in packets. She's film-star quality in that way. I can't describe it, but she's now got presence, which she didn't have when she was younger, and when you put the combination of presence and charisma together, you've got Jackie Kennedy.'

The late widow of John F. Kennedy, the most charismatic president the United States has ever known, found herself one of the most glamorous single women in the world following his assassination in 1963, but without the fortune to match her status. Her response to her plight, if we can call it that, was to rush into marriage with the Greek billionaire shipping magnate, Aristotle Onassis. Thanks to the Spencer family fortune and a handsome divorce settlement, Diana's prospects are considerably better than the widow Kennedy's were. And, in addition to her financial security, Diana can be assured of a continuing high profile in the media, according to Lord Archer.

'If you think that she is going to disappear after the divorce and Charles is going to become a charismatic popular figure, forget it,' he says. 'Diana's going to be there. Now I don't suggest for a moment that she is going to have the sort of headlines and the sort of coverage that she had as the wife of the future king, but she's still the mother of a future king, and she will still fascinate journalists because she will sell newspapers.'

So where does she go from here? Many feel it is time for her to duck out of the limelight and give herself a second chance in the marriage stakes. 'I think she'll try to have a new life of her own, put a line under the past and start again,' says Archer. 'In fact, I'm very confident that that's what she will do.'

Royal watchers speculate on two strategies for the Princess with no throne to look forward to. The first is to put herself into voluntary exile abroad, with New York tipped as the most likely bolt-hole. An apartment on Central Park would offer the appropriate degree of metropolitan chic, with Park Avenue an enticing focus for her shopping expeditions and social life. This would have two crucial disadvantages from Diana's point of view, however. She would see even less of her children, on whom she patently dotes, and she would soon miss the status afforded her by the constant attentions of the British media.

The alternative scenario is that she will stay in her homeland and settle down with a new husband. Despite her relative affluence it seems likely that the eligibility that goes with being a latter-day Jackie Kennedy would lure suitors of great wealth. As Lord Archer observes: 'Don't think because you've got to chapter three there aren't another 20 chapters to go. I'm a romantic by nature, as anyone who's read my books knows, so I hope that she's happily married and has more children.'

Mary Spillane reckons such a move is not so much a romantic dream as a practical necessity.

'I don't think she's going to survive very long on her own, she is so isolated,' she says. 'I think the best thing for her would be to get into a relationship and perhaps have a second family. But she seems hell bent on hanging on to this mother-of-the-heir thing, doesn't she? It's her raison d'être.'

Spillane argues that the Princess should become more domesticated and dismiss from her mind any thought of taking further revenge through the media. 'She shouldn't do any more television interviews,' she says. 'She should shut up and get out of the limelight because she is too unstable to handle it. It's all come out. The horrors of the Will Carling–Julia Carling mess. It's all so sordid. We don't want to know any more really. We know enough now. She can't explain any more. The explanations are too sad to listen to. So I would suggest that she just gets on with living and starts doing new things, developing herself outside the banal, narrow range of interests that she has now and be seen as much as possible with her boys and their friends and their families.'

But Diana clearly has no intention of bowing out of public life.

She has become a twentieth-century icon, with an appeal that crosses borders. In countries where people have no loyalty to her royal line, her activities are followed with obsessive interest. Apart from the blanket coverage she receives from Britain's tabloids, she is fêted everywhere from France and Germany to the United States and Canada. Travellers to remote villages in South America return with tales of how the locals were interested in only one aspect of British life, 'Lady Di'.

Mindful of this level of global celebrity, she chose her 1995 television interview to make a prime-time pitch for the role she saw for herself in the years ahead. 'I'd like to be an ambassador for this country,' she said. 'I'd like to represent this country abroad. As I have all this media interest, let's not just sit in this country and be battered by it. Let's take them, these people, out to represent this country and the good qualities of it abroad. When I go abroad we've got 60 to 90 photographers, just from this country, coming with me, so let's use it in a productive way to help this country.'

Asked on what grounds she thought she had the right to be an ambassador, she answered: 'I've been in a privileged position for 15 years. I've got tremendous knowledge about people and how to communicate. I've learned that I've got it, and I want to use it. And when I look at people in public life I'm not a political animal but I think the biggest disease the world suffers from in this day and age is the disease of people feeling unloved. And I know that I can give life for a minute, for half an hour, for a day, for a month, but I can give – I'm very happy to do that and I want to do that.'

Dr Dorothy Rowe reckons such a role would represent a useful 'transitional object' for Diana – something to see her through a painful period of adjustment in her life. 'I think the Queen of Hearts title will prove to be quite unrealistic,' she says. 'It's something she can't maintain, but it's not a bad transitional object – that's a phrase from Donald Winnicott, a wonderful child analyst. He would talk about things like when you were little you had a favourite toy or object that you held with you all the time, and it helped you get through the next difficult situation, and so it was a transitional object that got you from one point to the next. A lot of affairs can be transitional objects, people can be transitional objects.'

At first Diana's chances of being awarded such a transitional role looked good. Two weeks after her television interview, she made a highly successful trip to see President Carlos Menem in Argentina. Her host described her visit as 'exceptional, absolutely positive' and added: 'Diana managed to get her way to the heart of my people. She could be an excellent roving ambassador of goodwill, representing the UK in the rest of the world.'

In the months that followed the interview there was a conspicuous lack of progress in this direction, and her cause was not helped by her diplomatically insensitive visit to see Imran Khan and his wife, Jemima, the daughter of her friend Lady Annabel Goldsmith, in Pakistan four months later. Khan, who had denied any political ambitions, was nevertheless seen as a potentially serious threat to the re-election chances of President Benazir Bhutto, and, by paying court to him, Diana was perceived as committing a breach of protocol. State-run television refused to screen any footage of her arrival in Lahore, and the regime's paranoia about Khan's intentions proved justified when he announced his entry into politics following the bombing of his cancer hospital just weeks later.

Now the knives are out for the Princess at the Foreign Office. The mandarins there had an expensive brush with her spending habits on one of her earliest attempts to be an ambassador, a tour of the Gulf states in 1986. On her return she presented shocked civil servants with an £80,000 clothes bill for a wardrobe that had lasted just 16 days. The cost to the taxpayer of outfits by names such as Catherine Walker, Jacques Azagury and Paul Costello worked out at £2500 each. It was the same story when she paid her brief visit to the Khans, complete with an extensive wardrobe of *shalwar khameez*, the Pakistani national dress.

'We're talking half a dozen outfits, with matching shoes for each one, just for that one trip,' says Mary Spillane. 'When is she going to wear them again? She didn't need to do it. It actually looks very foolish for a Westerner to adopt native dress on a visit. Adopting signs of respect, as she's done in the past, like covering her head, wearing long sleeves and avoiding short dresses, of course. But do it with Western clothes rather than going native. That was just a way of getting a 12-page spread out of *Hello!*, and, of course, it worked.

A hell of a lot of thought went into that, and it shows what she does with her time.'

Such expenditure does not go down well with the bean counters at the Foreign Office. 'There was a real sucking in of breath over the dress bills Diana submitted for the Saudi tour she undertook with the Prince of Wales,' said a diplomat, who viewed with some trepidation the prospect of her working for the department. 'I suppose she could be asked to do the occasional trade visit,' he told *The Times*, adding waspishly: 'A retail fashion week in Salt Lake City, perhaps.'

Dr Sidney Crown reckons she may have alienated too many influential people by now to achieve her aim. 'At the time of the *Panorama* interview it seemed she might get what she wanted,' he says, 'but since that time all the people she would need to help her towards that, all the important people, whether politicians or royals, have come to distrust her. She would need to be trained for an ambassadorial role, and they're just not doing anything about that. She can't rush off to Indonesia, or wherever, and pretend that her visit does not have political significance as it did in Pakistan. If she's really going to be an ambassador, even an ambassador in inverted commas, I don't think her personality is such that she would be willing to learn from the people who would teach her how to be diplomatic. Being a diplomat takes an enormous amount of training and a lot of work in all sorts of places.'

She certainly has her doubters in the media. David Montgomery, chief executive of Mirror Group Newspapers, has reservations about whether she is up to the task. 'Who knows? She may be,' he says. 'I suppose if she met the right sort of man he might be able to do something for her, but with difficulty frankly.'

Even senior churchmen are prepared to make their views known on her unsuitability for a high-profile public role. 'I think she'll become a greater and greater irritant,' says the Venerable George Austin, Archdeacon of York. 'I think she'll just become an eccentric oddity. This Queen of Hearts thing will just come to look more and more ridiculous.'

He views her preoccupation with mediums and astrologers as 'crazy'. 'It's one of those things that has come over from America,' he says. 'We all catch the American disease for a while, everyone has to be counselled. There's no acceptance of personal responsibility. It's the Adam and Eve syndrome. God says: "Have you eaten from the tree from which I forbade you to eat?" and Adam replies: "Well, actually, God, yes, I have, but it was that woman you gave me, she gave it to me. You gave me the woman so it's your fault." It's the refusal to accept responsibility for anything we've done. You watch a football match, and when the goalkeeper lets a goal in, he immediately jumps up and points to others.'

It cannot be said, however, that Diana has not shown a hunger for self-improvement in the past, albeit one that concentrated to some extent on her own image. When she embarked on her royal career, her public speaking left a lot to be desired. Speeches were delivered in a monotone and failed to engage the audience in the way they do today. With characteristic single-mindedness she set about refining her technique. Actor Peter Settelen, a former star of *Coronation Street*, who was introduced to Diana by her one-time fitness trainer Carolan Brown, was enlisted to hone her vowels. Oliver Hoare later took her to the flat in the Albany, a prestigious apartment block close to Piccadilly Circus in London, to see the film star Terence Stamp, who agreed to give her voice-coaching. The actor, who achieved superstar status in the sixties with his role in *The Collector*, taught the Princess the importance of timing, pausing for emphasis and maintaining eye contact with those whom she was addressing.

'She has had coaching to get better at what she does,' says Mary Spillane, 'and the transformation from the inability to string more than three words together, even read notes, to that *Panorama* interview is a quantum leap that a lot of people can't make. A lot of women can't make that.'

But while Diana has got her marketing down to a fine art, many of the other qualities required by the travelling guardian angel appear to be missing.

'It seems unlikely that the Princess has the persistence and determination, which enable her sister-in-law, the Princess Royal, to do such an impressive job for the Save The Children Fund and other charities,' royal biographer Philip Ziegler once wrote. 'To trudge around malarial swamps or arid deserts, indifferent to discomfort or fatigue, without a worry about dignity or personal appearance, is not to be expected of Princess Diana.'

Apart from the demands it would make on her fastidiousness, it is clear that, intellectually, Diana is not a natural candidate for more formal ambassadorial tasks such as assimilating complex policy documents, negotiating treaties or wooing recalcitrant dictators. Her eyes visibly glaze over at the sight of paperwork. The woman who is more at home in a designer gown and high heels in a ballroom than donning fatigues and army boots to visit the scene of a bomb blast probably never envisaged that sort of job in any case. While she did not define fully the role she wanted, we can assume that it involves looking good and charming politicians and businessmen, with a visit to the sick and dying as part of the equation. It is telling that she chose the term 'Queen of people's hearts' and not servant of their needs. She appears to see herself as an informal global monarch, scattering her stardust worldwide and adding some lustre to her personal standing in the process.

To achieve this, however, she would be wise to restore some privacy to her private life. On her trip to see the Khans in Pakistan a reception in her honour was widely boycotted by many of the great and the good because, in that strictly Muslim country, many did not want to associate with a self-confessed adulteress.

And the fall-out from her private life has already affected aspects of her work in Britain. Guests at a lavish celebration to commemorate the 125th birthday of the British Red Cross in February 1996 were disappointed to find that instead of the Princess they had expected to see, they had to settle for television personality Cilla Black. There proved to be far-reaching ramifications for this uncharacteristic display of unreliability. Two months later a Red Cross spokesman said that its new Queen of Hearts was to be Liz Hurley, the Estée Lauder model and girlfriend of film star Hugh Grant. Diana remained as a vice-president of the organization, but it was clear that her role was less elevated.

But if an ambassadorial career looks out of the question, something else will have to take its place if Diana is not to fall into a spiral of discontent. 'She has to think of something to keep herself in the public eye, because otherwise she's going to get depressed,' says Dr Dennis Friedman. 'Unless, as I say, her therapy has helped her to be sufficiently self-assured and her self-esteem has become sufficiently robust that she no longer needs to be always on centre stage.' Without the fillip to her morale offered by such a role, Dr Friedman predicts a 'very difficult time' for the Princess. 'Rejection, it's all rejection,' he says. 'It must be awful for her.'

While her public role remains the subject of speculation, her home life is beginning to look more and more problematic. There is concern that her very public revelations about both her own love life and that of Charles could have a further effect on her children, already upset at their parents' split.

'What children want is to have parents who get along well together,' says Dr Dorothy Rowe, 'who provide for them well, who are there when they need them, but otherwise don't interfere in their lives, whose good sense and love they can rely on. And when we don't have that then we feel aggrieved because we haven't got perfect parents. These poor lads have got all this additional hoo-ha. It's not just a matter of seeing their mother pouring her heart out on television. To William and Harry their parents are immeasurably old, and old people having sex is disgusting. When you are 14, you certainly think that anyone in their thirties is over the hill and finished. But mum's looking quite good for her age. Dad? God, you know. And Camilla? Ugh!'

Quite how profound an effect this would have depends upon the durability of the boys' psyches. 'William, being the more sensitive one, is more likely to be harmed by what their mother said about her and their father's affairs,' says Dr Crown. 'Children learn, with great pain, to come to terms with things that happen when marriages or relationships break up. But some of them are harmed for a long time. It could make it more difficult for these young boys to make relationships in the future.'

In addition to their internal anxieties the boys might also find themselves the butt of teasing in the playground, says Dr Crown. 'I'm sure they would suffer, if not abuse, a lot of taunting,' he says. 'I think it's certainly harmful, but you can't say how permanent it is. That very much depends on the personality of the children and the figures that are there to support them, not only the parents but grandparents, aunts and teachers and so on.'

What no one doubts is Diana's devotion to her children even if, at times, she has a somewhat strange way of showing it. 'Yes, she's very concerned about them,' says Dr Dennis Friedman, author of *Inheritance: A Psychological History of the Royal Family*, 'because she can see what happened to her, and she doesn't want it to happen to them. She's not doing it [the *Panorama* programme] deliberately to embarrass them, these are unconscious patterns, which, as I pointed out in my book, run through all families from Victoria and Albert right the way through to the present ones and are unconsciously repeated.

'Although the last thing that she wants is for her children to suffer the way that she did, she's actually created the conditions in which they might. In other words, both come from a broken home now, both have parents who couldn't get on with each other etc. In fact they got sent away to boarding school just as she was. Whether they will be damaged depends on their personalities. If they're reasonably robust and happy with things they might be all right, but if they're rather fragile, as I think Charles and Diana themselves are, then they might not.'

Dr Robert Lefever reckons the boys would benefit from some therapy now. 'I look after children right the way down,' he says. 'I've had an eight year old in here, and we see the young families of all our patients because we will treat the entire family. There is a family equivalent of every anonymous fellowship. For teenagers there is Alateen – and would you believe it? – in the States they even have Alatot for the under-tens. And they can go along and share their experiences with each other.'

Dr Lefever believes the young Princes already qualify for membership of Alateen. 'Again I think they could be helped, not to prevent any addictive tendency they may have inherited, but at least to understand what is going on and to be aware that they will have a significantly higher risk than the population as a whole of developing addictive tendencies.'

What is certain is that as the years go by the small boys she once doted on will pass through adolescence and into adulthood, growing further away from their mother all the while. 'She's coming up to a time when her children are going to be drifting away naturally,' says psychologist Susan Quilliam. 'William is going to get a girlfriend, even if it is only a walk-in-the-park-holding-hands relationship. What does Diana do then? She's got a big life change coming up.'

At the same time her ability to alienate her peers seems to be becoming more and more marked. So where will this leave a divorced princess? Diana herself is putting a brave face on her predicament. 'I'm not really on my own,' she told *Panorama*. 'I've got wonderful friends, I've got my boys, I've got my work. It's just by living at Kensington Palace, obviously, it's a little bit isolating, but, you know, maybe we all feel like that.' She added: 'But I don't feel sorry for myself in any way. I've got my work that I choose to do, and I've got my boys, and I've got lots of opportunities coming up in the next year.'

The growing isolation, however, is one of the central fears of those who genuinely have Diana's best interests at heart. 'One of the problems I found on the two occasions when I was involved was that Diana didn't have a staff of people in the building for her,' says Lord Archer. 'Diana goes to bed on her own, and she gets lonely. And by nature she's someone who likes human beings. You've only got to see her cuddling children to see that. She likes human beings. Many of the Royal Family have been taught to keep human beings at a distance. Very lately they have actually talked to crowds, but walkabouts are a new thing for the Royal Family.

'If you came in here and said, "Jeffrey, you come here and sit on your own. We'll let you know when you can come out. It would be about once a fortnight. You must look your best, and you'll make one speech, and then you'll go home again" – I'd be a bloody nutcase.'

In off-the-record interviews others have expressed concern about Diana's lonely existence, for despite her claim about having 'wonderful friends' she is known to express a degree of suspicion about many of her intimates since her world starting falling apart. As Lord Archer told the authors: 'You may not be cracking up because you're not under any pressure, but you must show some sympathy and understanding for the fact she is.'

However, the pressure she is under need not necessarily bode ill for the future, according to Susan Quilliam. 'There are two possibilities,' she says. 'There is the optimistic one and the pessimistic one. The optimistic one is that she's basically between a rock and a hard place, and she's sorting herself out. The pessimistic one, which worries me, is that she's a blamer, and she's moving through a situation where she's blaming herself less and blaming other people more. A good example of this is how she will make a friendship and then switch the blame from herself to the friend and so alienate him or her. Basically she has decided she can't trust anybody at all, so she's progressively cutting off – and, in psychotherapy terms, it's a very dangerous sign.

'The more you can get somebody integrated into society, the less you are likely to get extreme symptoms. Somebody who is on their own can get into a loop where one harmful thought, one critical thought, leads to another, and the person just goes round and round in circles. If the person is interacting with other people, they will often be a lot better. The other people will give them something different to think about, they'll give them more input, they'll bring them out of the loop. A simple example would be arriving at the office in a really bad mood after an awful drive to work. You walk into the office, somebody interacts with you, and five minutes later you've forgotten about the bad journey. But if you enter a totally empty office, you might well sit there and stew for 20 minutes because you go into this mental loop. One of the important things is to keep your support system going, get drawn out, interact with people.'

As one expert puts it: 'Diana has actually moved to a stage where she's blaming others, and her very power is isolating her. She doesn't actually have anybody any more, with the possible exception of Susie Orbach, who can say, "Don't be silly." And Diana will soon get fed up with her. If there is an emotional component to their relationship, and it looks very much as though there is, she may well start to blame her.

'She has put Orbach on a pedestal, and one of the few certainties in an uncertain world is that people who are raised so high either fall off or get pushed off. When that happens Diana will go, "Oh God, you weren't so wonderful after all." She'll walk over her and on to somebody else.'

Psychiatrist Dr Sidney Crown likens this withdrawal into the self to the concept of 'anomie', defined by the sociologist Emile

Durkheim. According to Durkheim, a society that lacks clear-cut norms to govern human aspirations and moral conduct is characterized by anomie, which means 'lack of rules' or 'normlessness'. This situation can lead to alienation from friends, family and society at large and eventually reaches a point where death is seen as the only option. 'I wouldn't say I wouldn't be surprised if she committed suicide, because everyone would be surprised,' says Dr Crown. 'But I think the Palace and its advisors, whoever they are, must be concerned and would try, in some way that wouldn't make it obvious to her, to keep an eye on her.

'As to whether she would actually take an overdose, for example, my answer is that I don't think she would. But she could do something that would get her killed by somebody outside, or put herself at danger in some other way by being reckless. I've thought about this, particularly in terms of the IRA. I made some sort of grim joke with my wife about it, that there is nothing Diana would like more, in a sense, than to go out as a martyr. All the suggestions have been that she is being particularly stupid in not obeying her bodyguards. I think there is a bit of her, whether it's conscious or unconscious, that would like to go out at the top, and, of course, she would actually if some IRA bloke knocked her off. Paradoxically, her status in public opinion would rise.'

Although he reckons the thought of abandoning her children would prevent Diana from taking the ultimate step, Dr Crown is convinced she has 'probably' considered it. 'It's a complicated question,' he says, 'but I don't think she'd do it in the sense of putting a gun to her head, taking an overdose or cutting her wrists properly.'

The potential dangers posed by Diana's determination to go it alone were highlighted on the night of 23 March 1996, when the BMW she was driving along Cromwell Road in west London collided with a Porsche sent careering into her path by an incompetent parking attendant. With her rented car too damaged to be driven from the scene, the woman was forced to find a taxi to take her to the nearest police station.

The argument that Diana might take the ultimate step is given added credence by the allegation that she has attempted suicide in the past. Her biographer Andrew Morton, acting on information supplied indirectly by the Princess herself, reported that she once threw herself down a flight of stairs at Sandringham and, on another occasion, during a heated argument with Prince Charles, slashed at her chest and thighs with a penknife.

Dr Dorothy Rowe points out that people who have made attempts on their lives however feeble are more likely to commit suicide than those who have not. 'The old idea that if people say they are going to kill themselves, they won't, is quite wrong. People who kill themselves usually say in their suicide notes, "But nobody's taken any notice."'

Dr Rowe adds: 'People can feel so desperate that the feeling of wanting to kill yourself can come over you very, very suddenly, very powerfully, and you just do whatever's available to do. Sometimes what you do isn't sufficient to kill you, and sometimes it is. A large number of car crashes on our roads occur when somebody's driving along and is overwhelmed by the feeling, I must kill myself, and they drive into a barrier. There are lots of reports of cars just going out of control, and when it comes to the autopsy it becomes clear the driver didn't suffer a heart attack.'

Reviewing Diana's circumstances today Dr Rowe concludes that her life lies, to some degree, in the hands of the Palace: 'If the Palace made it impossible for her to have contact with her sons and prevented her from being able to play any significant part in her sons' lives; if the divorce settlement proves to be insufficient to keep her in the manner to which she has become accustomed; if she failed to form any close friendships or any good relationships; if people were taking advantage of her and then betraying her; if she was no longer involved in this reciprocal relationship of visiting people and people being pleased, and there was nothing else in her life to give her a sense of achievement: then she would feel so lonely and so depressed and so shamed by everything going so much against her, that she could feel the only way to assuage her guilt and her shame would be to kill herself.

'We all want to feel that our life has some significance, and when we lose that we feel that terrible emptiness, when there is no point going on. Quite often in those situations you don't actually have to do anything to kill yourself. You give up, and you die. When every bit of you, body and soul feels there is no point, there is nothing to live for, you don't have to kill yourself. Every day in hospitals there are people dying who have simply given up.

'A very good friend of mine is a Supreme Court judge in the Northern Territory [Australia]. When she first went up there to work as a chief magistrate she would quite often be holding a coroner's court over a perfectly healthy, dead male Aborigine, and this would be someone who'd broken the tribal rule and had been expelled. He'd just gone off into the bush and died. It doesn't even involve casting a spell. It's just a matter of telling people, "This is the structure of the world, and you have no place in it." The Palace could do that to Diana, and she knows it because she has seen them do it to other, lesser people.'

Dr Robert Lefever believes that Diana has not yet reached the low point that all addicts must reach before they are ready to admit that a treatment programme is essential to their recovery. 'The process of surrender is a process of exhaustion, of loneliness and of misery,' he says. 'You go through it and, in your deep inner loneliness, you say, "I can't go on like this." Now, at that point you either contemplate suicide, or you get better through acknowledging that your way doesn't work, and you're just going to have to ask for help. Now the tragedy of being someone like the Princess of Wales is that if you ask for help the whole world is on your doorstep. Everybody wants to make his or her name being your guru. I feel very sad for her in that she has a very difficult job in finding people who are able to look after her who are not going to use her.'

So might she try to kill herself? 'You can never tell,' he replies. 'It's a perfectly realistic question. Addicts do have a very high incidence of suicide, and therefore it's a perfectly reasonable concern for any person who has addictive behaviour. The major cause of death in addicts are suicide and accidents. We don't just die of ruptured oesophaguses or drug overdoses or whatever.'

Agony aunt Claire Rayner is unwilling to venture an opinion on the suicide issue but does say: 'Let's just say, if it hit the news one day I wouldn't be in the least bit surprised.'

Already there are the first signs that Diana is as Dr Rowe puts it being excluded from the tribe. Her name was pointedly left off the Queen's list of guests for a private dinner party to celebrate her seventieth birthday in April 1996. Gallingly for Diana, Prince Edward's girlfriend, Sophie Rhys-Jones, was invited.

The Princess on the edge has a choice: she can either topple into the abyss or pull herself back from the brink. According to more than one of our experts, her bulimia may be in remission, but the illness is manifesting itself in other ways, and they fear a spiral of decline as she becomes more and more obsessive, driving away those who might help her in the process. Her chances of fulfilling her aspiration to be 'queen of people's hearts' look more remote by the day as her increasingly desperate attempts to curry favour with the 'people' backfire.

Her sons are growing up, and, as their independence increases, so she will be left without the one source of unconditional love she had left. In the face of this, they say, she has resorted to talk cures that are conducted on her terms and offer no realistic hope of resolving her crisis. Their prognosis is bleak, and they suggest her only chance of salvation lies in accepting the hopelessness of her situation, retreating from the public gaze and coming to terms with her inner torment through a commitment to more intensive treatment before it is too late.

Other specialists see grounds for optimism. They argue that she has fought bravely against the psychological torment imposed upon her by the royal household and is taking a responsible attitude to her problems by airing them through a programme of psychotherapy. Even 'the enemy' must now be hoping that she will find the inner peace and happiness that has so far eluded her.

INDEX